A HISTORY OF THE DRESS

OF THE

BRITISH SOLDIER,

FROM THE

EARLIEST PERIOD TO THE PRESENT TIME.

BY

LIEUT.-COLONEL JOHN LUARD

Illustrated with Fifty Drawings

– 1852 –

The Naval & Military Press Ltd

published in association with

ROYAL ARMOURIES

Published by
The Naval & Military Press Ltd
Unit 10 Ridgewood Industrial Park,
Uckfield, East Sussex,
TN22 5QE England
Tel: +44 (0) 1825 749494
Fax: +44 (0) 1825 765701
www.naval-military-press.com

in association with

ROYAL
ARMOURIES

In reprinting in facsimile from the original, any imperfections are inevitably reproduced and the quality may fall short of modern type and cartographic standards.

PREFACE.

There is a droll saying, that, with a series of old newspapers, some paste, and a pair of scissors, a very entertaining book can be made! No doubt there is truth in this; for what is history, but extracts from the works of various authors, collected by patient research, arranged in chronological order, with remarks and observations by the writer, and perhaps embellished with illustrations? The "History of the Dress of the British Soldier" has been compiled in this way; and I shall at once put the reader in possession of the authorities from whom I have gained my information, rather than fill the body of the volume with notes and references, which, though very necessary in many works, are always a disagreeable interruption, and are not required in this. The works that I am most indebted to are the following:—

Planché's "History of British Costume."

"The History of Dress from the Earliest Period till the Close of the Eighteenth Century." By F. W. Fairholt, F.S.A.

"The History of the British Army." By Grose.

"A Critical Inquiry into Ancient Armour as it existed in Europe, but particularly in England, from the Norman Conquest to the Reign of Charles II." By Sir S. Meyrick.

"The Illustrations of the Armour and Ancient Arms at Goodrich Court." By Skelton.

Gough's "Sepulchral Monuments."

Stothard's "Monumental Effigies."

"Notes and Recollections of a Professional Life." By the late William Ferguson, Esq., M.D.

Anecdotes have been taken from Froissart, and reference has been made to Montfaucon's "Antiquites Expliquée," as well as to other works.

Several of the drawings have been made from the armour in the Tower of London, and some from monumental effigies; than which, it is considered, there cannot be more faithful representations of the dress of those who lie buried beneath them. By these means there is no great difficulty in tracing the costume of men of rank to a remote period. Many monumental effigies have been broken and disfigured by Cromwell's ruthless soldiers; nevertheless, there remain sufficient in a tolerably perfect state, of various dates, to carry us back to the Norman Conquest. There also exists splendid armour of men of rank, of different periods, which puts us in possession of the costumes of those early days; but it is not easy to ascertain how soldiers of inferior rank were clad, because they were engaged by men of wealth and power to serve their sovereign for a limited time, or for a particular expedition; and when the period of service had expired, or the expedition was over, they fell back again into citizen or agriculturist, and their war dresses, being of little value, were neglected, and went to decay. Very little respecting soldiers' clothing occurs in history, or in records of early date. Formerly there was no regular uniform; and though there are instances of the Government clothing the soldiers, yet, generally, the armour they wore was their own individual property, and kept in consequence of their feudal tenures. Charles the Sixth of France first introduced standing armies in Europe. Our early kings do not appear to have had even a body-guard. Under these circumstances, the exact dress of the lower grades of soldiers, during the earliest periods of our history, is scarcely to be ascertained. I have, however, in Plate XI., drawn an archer and a cross-bowman of the time of Henry V. The latter is copied from a drawing of Sir S. Meyrick's; the former is designed from the descriptions I have read of that dress. But these were not soldiers of the lowest grade. I have also attempted portraits of the Norman soldiers at the time of the Conquest, trusting more to that curious piece of work, the Bayeux tapestry, than any other representations. In Henry the Eighth's and Elizabeth's time we have drawings of soldiers. The uniform of the British army can scarcely be said to have commenced before the eighteenth century.

From the year 1809, when I joined the army, I have trusted to my own journals and sketches of the numerous changes which have been made in the dress of our soldiers. During the Peninsular War, I wore the heavy dragoon cocked-hat, as well as the heavy dragoon helmet; at the battle of Waterloo, the light dragoon shako; at the siege and capture of Bhurtpore, in India, the lancer cap. Since that time, both in England and in India, I have worn the staff cocked-hat. I may, therefore, fairly be allowed to criticise those head-dresses with which I have been many years familiar. If I have taken the same liberty with others, with which I have not been on the same intimate terms, it is from having received faithful reports of them from persons on whose judgment I can rely.

Many persons may be disappointed in the drawings of this volume, because they are not coloured. After much consideration, I came to the decision, that a distinct outline would more clearly show the forms of the various dresses than any other method which could be adopted. I beg to call the attention of those who might wish for coloured prints, to the costumes of Sir S. Meyrick's " Critical Inquiry into Ancient Armour as it existed in Europe, but more particularly in England, from the Norman Conquest to the Reign of Charles II.," where the illustrations are blurred and obscured by colour, and the outlines disfigured, conveying a very indistinct idea of what is intended; and request they will compare them with Skelton's clear and well-defined outlines of the "Armour and Ancient Arms at Goodrich Court." A coloured print is very seldom effective, even when well done; and it is almost impossible to represent the beautiful lights, shades, and reflections of armour. I do not presume that my outlines can be compared with Skelton's, but I trust that they are sufficiently distinct and correct to convey a just idea of the dresses described. Moreover, it is not the colour of the dress of our soldiers that I am most anxious about; it is the appropriateness of their garb, arms, and equipment, to the purposes of war.

I scarcely expect this volume to be an ornament to a drawing-room table; but I confess I am most anxious that it should be read by those interested in the welfare of the army, and by those in authority; not that I am vain enough to believe that which I have written will be implicitly followed, but I may have stated some facts, and given some hints, which will be heeded, and prove beneficial to the army; more particularly at this moment, when there is a feeling amongst most military men, that our army is not sufficiently well clothed, equipped, and armed.

Although I have been long anxious to write on this subject, I should have been glad if an abler pen and pencil had been employed. There seemed no prospect of this; therefore I have attempted the subject, which is certainly one of considerable importance to the army. My suggestions may not be approved of by many; it would be wonderful if they were, for perhaps there is nothing which admits of a greater variety of fancy and taste than dress; but I am convinced that every hint on the subject, given by experienced military men, is useful. My object, it will be seen, in this volume is to get rid of every incumbrance that may oppress the soldier, whether from the weight of his arms and knapsack, or from being clogged with superfluous straps, buttons, and tassels, and every inconvenient part of dress not adapted to the purposes of war. My feeling is, that no part of a soldier's dress should be merely ornamental; every thing that is appropriate and efficient for its purpose can be made handsome.

Convinced that a volume of this kind could not be published without considerable loss, unless done by subscription, I have adopted this method of publication. I am much flattered by the ready way in which my friends have met my wishes, and beg particularly to thank those who have kindly added their opinions on the subject to their subscriptions; many of the former are those of officers of high rank and experience, and carry with them weight, and express feelings which are very general. The following are extracts from their letters; the first is from an experienced officer, high in rank, who has served in every quarter of the globe, and is the hero of a hundred fights. He writes:—"During my long service, I never recollect the dress of the army being such as would ensure to the poor soldier on service comfort or convenience; the ornamental has been the study of those who had the direction of these matters. The late Sir William Meadows said, 'All men have fancy, few have taste;' and unfortunately the comfort and convenience of the soldier has been quite lost sight of in the anxiety of these fancy people to show their taste, which, by-the-by, has generally been very bad. The jackets of the men were at one time short, and cut off close to the hips (to look smart), so that no protection was afforded to those parts which (particularly on service) should be defended from wet and cold."

Another officer writes:—"I only hope your work may have the effect of inducing the authorities to give the soldier a dress and equipment that may be at the same time useful, comfortable, and handsome. As it is, it appears to be the sole object to make the dress as inconvenient and uncomfortable as possible; and in the case of the poor infantry, as hideous as can well be conceived.

"A light, neat, comfortable head-dress, a narrow pliable stock of some soft material, a loose frock coat to cover the loins and thighs, to come down within an inch and a half of the knee, and to be made large enough to admit of a comfortable waistcoat with sleeves under it, in the winter months at home, and in America, and other cold climates; and to be worn without the waistcoat in summer at home, and in warm climates. The knapsack and pouch should be improved; in short, the whole thing wants altering. If an infantry soldier has to step over a drain two feet broad, he has to put one hand to his cap to keep it on his head, and his other to his pouch; and what becomes of his musket!"

Now let us see what a cavalry man says. "It is very advisable in progressing to know what has been done before, and by what steps we have arrived at the present order of things, that we may not risk for novelty sake that which is really no novelty, but has been tried and found wanting. I think while you point out the past, you may as well venture on a model for the future, avoiding all the inconvenience of the past. I can find no costume for a horseman so good as the loose overall and jacket of the hussar made easy in the arms; a good cloak at his saddle-bow, and a light waterproof over-coat with sleeves, which might be laid on his valise; as little gold lace as you please; a low busby, strongly built, that would save his head from a blow—a less abundant kit."

Another cavalry officer writes: "My own opinion is, that in our small army we should have no distinction of light and heavy cavalry, which, after all, is only in the red coat and brass hat, two things the sooner we are rid of the better. The general dress should be that of the old light dragoon as he went out to the Peninsula, with some slight improvement. But the chief point should be to have a fixed costume for the different climates we are liable to be sent to: for instance, what can be more absurd than a regiment in Canada and one at the Cape wearing the same dress?

yet this is supposed to be done. The King's dragoon guards wore in Canada a kind of busby, with blue pea-jackets, and long boots lined with sheepskin in the winter; very good and sensible, and quite indispensable, but most assuredly not according to regulation. The seventh hussars had only to put on the large sheepskin-lined boots with their warm pelisse, and they were well clothed; a proof of the advantage of the light over the heavy dress. A brass helmet was found not serviceable in Africa by the seventh dragoon guards when that regiment was at the Cape. Whatever may be the dress selected for dragoons, it should have nothing on the shoulders, the idea of protection is absurd; did any man in your old regiment, the sixteenth light dragoons, with the old dress, get more hurts than when it was changed? I would have all our dragoons, light dragoons, and, if you will it to call them so, keeping the lancers and hussars as at present, who are light troops, making them all go to India in their turn."

A person of rank says: "This is a subject which has met with less attention than it deserves, and you will do the British army good service in directing attention to it. I think the foppery and folly of former times has made people shy of approaching it; but there is nothing in this to deter one from treating it seriously, as it ought to be treated. In other countries, great modifications in the soldiers' dress and equipments have been introduced; and if this was wise and reasonable where the troops are not exposed to the great changes of climate, and fatigue of all kinds, which ours have to undergo, how much more is it required in the British army? I am aware that these very changes of climate make it difficult to suggest a uniform dress and equipment for our soldiers; but this is the very reason why the subject should be approached by those whose experience in different parts of the world entitles their opinion to respect. If only an equipment for European climates were required, probably the present Prussian system is as good as could be adopted; their motto seems to be, that nothing is ornamental in a soldier's dress and equipment which is not useful."

A guardsman writes: "I hope you will say nothing against the bearskin cap. I am very glad the subject has been thus taken up, and I wish you every success."

A very old friend—"I am delighted to subscribe to your book, and conclude that I shall form a conspicuous character in your publication in the costume I assumed in the year 1785."

An officer of rank, who has served long in India, writes: "I hope you mean to suggest the expediency of allowing the general introduction of regimental white jackets for undress parade, and ordinary duties in India, for the officers as well as the soldiers."

Another adds—"It is rather cruel upon the service to hand down to posterity the lavender-coloured trousers, which the unfortunate infantry are now condemned to wear, in addition to the shell jacket and the very ugly shako. From the different climates our army are obliged to serve in, it is impossible to combine utility with uniformity; good taste we can never expect."

A more than ordinary observant correspondent writes: "I shall be very glad if you dedicate a portion of your work to the dress of our soldiers in the colonies; I am satisfied this has not been sufficiently attended to by the authorities. I have, myself, seen the Spanish, French, and Danish troops in the West Indies much more healthy than our own, from great attention to their comfort in their dress. I am not able to give you any information on the subject, nor have I any drawings, but you are aware that, as regards dress, the whole body of civilians in the tropics appear in loose white jackets and trousers, and a light skull-cap; and, if my memory serves me, the shakos and red coats of our troops were not altered in our West India colonies."

A civilian tells me: "I have been staying a short while this summer with the fifty-second in Limerick barracks; and I should say, the ugliest head-piece, and integuments for the lower man, you will have to pourtray, will be the present infantry cap and light blue trousers."

A cavalry officer says: " I hope you will dwell on the madness of our soldiers wearing leather caps under a tropical sun."

A very old military friend, and distinguished officer, has mentioned, that he thinks " such a work as this will have no effect, but to make young officers dissatisfied with their present dress." I beg to state that nothing is further from my wish; I have ever been a determined stickler, for conforming in the minutest particular, to the regulations on dress, and have always expressed extreme dislike to every attempt made at regimental alteration by the taste or fancy of any officer, and which I still think most objectionable. I trust that I cannot be misunderstood on this point. It is true, that I have found fault with the arms, dress, and equipment of our army, but I have done so generally and on principle; with the earnest desire not only to render service to our gallant troops, but to benefit our country.

Another friend has stated " that nothing is desirable in a soldier's dress which interferes with his appearance; that no extent of utility in any article can compensate him for becoming an object of ridicule in the opinion of the people by wearing it." I cannot accede to this observation: certainly it may be inconvenient to wear for years many parts of military equipment which are only useful on the day of battle, and that battle may only last a few hours, and be the only fight the soldier witnesses during his life; whilst others carry what they may deem cumbrous appointments during the whole period of their military career, useful only in war, without once having seen a shot fired in anger. But these are not good reasons for allowing the soldier to give up any portion of that equipment which may be only required in war, and at the moment of battle;

nor for decorating him with any splendid dress which would be found most objectionable in the hour of trial.

At the same time, there is no reason why military dress should not unite utility and beauty; but if this is impracticable, there can be no question that those parts of dress suited to the purposes of war, however frightful, should be adopted in preference to others unfit for those purposes, though very beautiful.

The ridicule of the people is a momentary ebullition, arising more from novelty than from other causes, and subsides when the eye is no longer a stranger to the object of excitement; otherwise, the little boys would run after the guardsmen when they appear in the streets of London, and shout at their overwhelming, preposterous, hideous bearskin caps.

With great diffidence I now commit my volume to the criticism of the public, more particularly to those of military men, trusting, however, to their kind feelings, and hoping that the errors may be palliated by the good intentions of the Author.

CONTENTS.

	PAGE
Ancient British Period	1
The Roman British Period	2
Anglo-Saxon Period	4
The Normans	7
Reigns of William II., Henry I., and Stephen	9
Henry II., Richard I., and John	12
Henry III.	17
Edward I.	19
Edward II.	20
Edward III.	22
Richard II.	26
Henry IV.	28
Henry V.	31
Henry VI.	36
Edward IV.	40
Edward V.	45
Richard III.	45
Henry VII.	47
Henry VIII.	53
Edward VI.	64
Mary I.	66
Elizabeth	69
James I.	73
Charles I.	75
The Commonwealth	79

CONTENTS.

	PAGE
Reign of Charles II.	83
James II.	89
William and Mary	91
Queen Anne	93
George I. and George II.	95
George III.	97
George IV.	107
William IV.	108
Queen Victoria	109
The Armies of India	112
Review of the Dress of Past Times	120
Fire-arms	136
Marching	145
Formation of the Army	149
Explanation of various parts of Armour	167
Description of Defensive Armour for the Body	169
Armour for Horses	171

LIST OF PLATES.

NO.		TO FACE PAGE
I.	Roman Soldiers	3
II.	Anglo-Saxons	6
III.	Norman Soldiers	7
IV.	Helmets. B.C. 870.—A.D. 400.	9
V.	Knights of the time of Henry II.	13
VI.	Crusaders	14
VII.	Specimens of Mail	16
VIII.	Helmets and Armour	18
IX.	Knights of the time of Edward I. II. and III.	21
X.	Richard II. and two Knights	26
XI.	An Archer and Crossbowman. A.D. 1399—1422	34
XII.	Henry VI. and Knight	39
XIII.	Mounted Knights. A.D. 1461—1483.	41
XIV.	Knights in Armour—time of Richard III. and Henry VII.	47
XV.	Helmets, from A.D. 1096—1520	52
XVI.	Armour in the Tower belonging to Henry VIII.	55
XVII.	Russet Armour in the Tower—time of Edward VI.	64
XVIII.	A Demi-lancer, and puffed and ribbed Armour, and a Yeoman of the Guard	68
XIX.	Archers, Demi-lancer, Pikeman, and Arquebusier—time of Elizabeth	72
XX.	James I., Henry Prince of Wales, and a Soldier armed with a caliver	74
XXI.	Cuirassier, Arquebusier, and Dragoon. A.D. 1625—1649	77
XXII.	Oliver Cromwell and the Earl of Essex	81
XXIII.	Cuirassier, an Arquebusier, and a Musqueteer. A.D. 1660—1685	84

LIST OF PLATES.

NO.		TO FACE PAGE
XXIV.	Lord Fairfax and an Antick. A.D. 1646	87
XXV.	Helmets, from A.D. 1558—1685	88
XXVI.	The Duke of Monmouth and Lord Grey	90
XXVII.	The Duke of Schomberg and General Caillemot	92
XXVIII.	Soldiers. A.D. 1701—1714	94
XXIX.	Heavy and Light Dragoons and Guardsmen. A.D. 1714—1760	95
XXX.	Officer of 4th Dragoons. A.D. 1785	99
XXXI.	George III., Heavy and Light Dragoon Officers, and a Fusilier. A.D. 1805	100
XXXII.	Heavy and Light Dragoons, with Lemonade Man. A.D. 1811	101
XXXIII.	Officers of Heavy Dragoons, Infantry and Staff. A.D. 1811	102
XXXIV.	Officer's Dress in 1812	103
XXXV.	Dress of Officers of the French Army. A.D. 1814	104
XXXVI.	An Officer of Lancers. Infantry and Staff. A.D. 1817	106
XXXVII.	A Lifeguardsman, Heavy Dragoon, and Lancer. A.D. 1824	108
XXXVIII.	A Highlander, and the Dress of the 74th Regiment worn at the Cape of Good Hope. A.D. 1851	110
XXXIX.	The Cavalry of A.D. 1852	111
XL.	The Infantry of A.D. 1852	111
XLI.	A Native Officer, and Sepoys of the Company's Army. A.D. 1757	114
XLII.	A Sepoy, and two of Skinner's Horse. A.D. 1826	114
XLIII.	Bengal Regular Cavalry, Irregular Cavalry, Goorka, and Infantry. A.D. 1842	117
XLIV.	Hats and Helmets. A.D. 1625—1824	119
XLV.	A Dragoon appointed as Marshal Saxe proposed, and a saddle	126
XLVI.	Head-dresses of two Ladies of A.D. 1782, and those of a Guardsman and Horse-artilleryman of A.D. 1851	130
XLVII.	Present Helmets and Caps, and those proposed	163
XLVIII.	Proposed Dress for Infantry	165
XLIX.	Full Dress for Officers	166
L.	Proposed Dress for Cavalry	166

LIST OF SUBSCRIBERS.

The Royal Library, Windsor (two copies).
His Grace the Duke of Beaufort.
His Grace the Duke of Roxburghe (two copies).
Her Grace the Dowager Duchess of Roxburghe.
Field Marshal the Marquis of Anglesea, K.G., G.C.B., G.C.H.
The Earl of Amherst, G.C.H.
The Earl of Verulam.
The Earl of Yarborough.
The Earl of Ellenborough, G.C.B.
General Viscount Combermere, G.C.B., G.C.H.
Viscount Emlyn, M.P.
The Lord Bishop of Salisbury.
Colonel Lord de Ros.
Lord Dinorben.
Lieut.-General Earl Cathcart, K.C.B.
Lord Elphinstone, G.C.H.
General Lord Saltoun, K.C.B., G.C.H.
General Viscount Gough, G.C.B.
Lord Charles Wellesley.
General Viscount Lord Lorton.
General Lord Charles Manners, K.C.B.
Lady Nelson and Bronti.

xviii LIST OF SUBSCRIBERS.

Lady Buxton.
Lord Tenterden.
Lieut.-General Lord Fitzroy Somerset, K.C.B.
Right Hon. H. Pierrepont.
Sir Charles Anderson, Bart.
Sir Frederick Bathurst, Bart.
Sir Montague Cholmeley, Bart.
Sir John D'Oyly, Bart.
Sir William de Bathe, Bart.
Colonel Sir J. Ord Honyman, Bart., Grenadier Guards.
General Sir Edward Kerrison, Bart., G.C.B.
Sir John Nelthorpe, Bart.
Sir H. Roper.
Lieut.-General Sir Thomas M'Mahon, Bart., K.C.B.
Sir Charles Rowan, Bart., C.B.
Admiral Sir Thomas Pasley, Bart., R.N.
Captain Sir Warwick Morshead, Bart., 6th Dragoons.
Sir Trevor Wheler, Bart.
Lieut.-General Sir John Brown, K.C.B.
General Sir William Keir Grant, K.C.B., G.C.H.
Lieut.-General Brotherton, C.B.
General William Campbell, C.B.
Lieut.-General Duffy, C.B.
Lieut.-General Egerton, C.B.
Lieut.-General Sir de Lacy Evans, K.C.B., M.P.
Lieut.-General George Hunter, C.B.
Lieut.-General Sir George Scovell, K.C.B.
Major-General Lawrence, C.B.
Lieut.-General the Hon. Henry Lygon, C.B.
Major-General Love, C.B., commanding South Wales district.
Lieut.-General the Hon. H. Murray, C.B.
General Sir Charles Napier, G.C.B.
Lieut.-General Nicolls, C.B.
Lieut.-General James Hay, C.B. (two copies).
Lieut.-General M'Leod, C.B.
Lieut.-General Sir George Pollock, K.C.B., G.C.B.
Major-General Lovell, C.B.

LIST OF SUBSCRIBERS.

Lieut.-General Sleigh, C.B.
Major-General Taylor, C.B.
Major-General Riddell, C.B., commanding in Scotland.
Major-General Sir Charles Odonnell, K.C.B.
Major-General Baron Osten, K.H.
Sir Roderick Impey Murcheson, M.A., F.R.S., G.C., S.S., President of the
    Royal Geographical Society.
Colonel Sir Edward Cust, K.C.H., F.R.S.
Sir Robert Comyn.
The Dean of Salisbury.
Rev. and Hon. F. P. Bouverie.
Colonel the Hon. P. Cust.
Lieut.-Colonel the Hon. J. York Scarlet, 5th Dragoon Guards (two copies).
Lieut.-Colonel the Hon. C. Wrottesley.
Lieutenant the Hon. H. L. B. Rowley, 6th Dragoons.
Captain the Hon. R. Lawley, 2nd Life Guards.

Lieut.-Colonel Ainslie, 7th Dragoon Guards.
Major Archer, 16th Lancers.
Major Ainslie, 21st Fusiliers.
Dr. Alderson, M.D., F.R.S.
H. Angelo, Esq. (two copies).
J. Armytage, Esq.
Dr. Auchinleck, M.D., 82nd regiment.
Major-General Buckley, C.B.
Colonel Bouverie, Royal Horse Guards (three copies).
Colonel Beresford, Deputy Adjutant-General, Cork.
Wilberforce Bird, Esq.
Major Borton, 9th Regiment.
W. B. Bayly, Esq.
Edward Bouverie, Esq.
Rev. Thomas Bacon.
Charles, Brodie, Esq.
Captain Edwin Burnaby, Grenadier Guards.
Lieut.-Colonel Boileau, Bengal Engineers.
Edward Baker, Esq.
William Belli, Esq.

Lieutenant Hugh L. Barton, 6th Dragoons.
Lieutenant Barron, 82nd Regiment.
Lieut.-Colonel Cartwright
Colonel Chatterton, K.H., S.F., M.P., High Sheriff, County Cork.
Colonel R. Craycroft.
Colonel Childers, C.B.
Colonel U. L. Clowes.
Colonel Charlewood.
Major-General Hare Clargis.
Captain Cromelin, Bengal Engineers.
H. Chamier, Esq.
Captain H. Cholmeley, 27th Regiment.
T. Colby, Esq.
Philip Cazenove, Esq.
Major Chase.
John Cazenove, Esq.
John Dalton, Esq.
Colonel Hastings Doyle, Limerick.
Colonel C. Dalton, Royal Artillery.
Henry Dalbiac, Esq.
William Dalbiac, Esq.
Mrs. Downes.
William Dick, Esq.
Colonel Dixon, Scotch Fusilier Guards.
Major-General Everard.
F. J. Egerton, Esq. (two copies).
Captain Elmhurst, 9th Regiment.
Walker Ewer, Esq.
Captain Edwardes.
Dr. Fitton, M.D., F.R.S.
Captain F. W. J. Fitzwigram, 6th Dragoons.
J. Lockyer Freeston, Esq.
Charles Freeling, Esq.
Clayton Freeling, Esq.
Dr. Fowler, M.D.
W. R. Farmer, Esq., 82nd Regiment.
Lieut.-Colonel Garrett, 46th Regiment.

Colonel Gordon.
Arbuthnot Guthrie, Esq.
J. Golden, Esq.
Colonel Greaves.
Arthur Gregory, Esq.
Alexander Greig, Esq.
J. H. Glover, Esq., Librarian, Royal Library, Windsor.
William T. Græme, Esq.
John Gordon, Esq., 82nd Regiment.
Captain Edward Gwynne.
Colonel Hugonin.
Lieut.-Colonel Hodge, 4th Dragoon Guards.
Captain Harrison, 63rd Regiment.
G. F. Heneage, Esq.
Edward Heneage, Esq.
Henry Bacon Hickman, Esq.
Robert W. Hughes, Esq.
Lieutenant E. D'Arcy, 6th Dragoons.
J. R. Hay, Esq.
Colonel Hall, 1st Life Guards.
Captain Halliday, 82nd Regiment.
R. Haywood, Esq., 82nd Regiment.
R. G. Hubback, Esq.
George Jones, Esq.
Major Jones, 11th Hussars.
Henry Jacob, Esq.
W. G. Jennings, Esq.
J. P. Jarvis, Esq., 82nd Regiment.
Philip Jones, Esq.
J. Knight, Esq
The Rev. Charles Le Bas.
Charles Le Bas, Esq., East India Company's Service.
C. B. Luard, Esq.
Captain R. Luard, Royal Artillery.
Henry Luard, Esq.
Rev. Edward Luard.
Rev. Octavius Luard.

LIST OF SUBSCRIBERS.

William Luard, Esq.
Thomas Lloyd, Esq.
Captain Lewis Lloyd.
Major Lewis.
Captain Brownlow Layard.
Sidney Lawrence, Esq.
J. Langshaw, Esq.
Major Lowe.
Cornwal Legh, Esq.
Lieut.-Colonel Lawrenson, 17th Lancers.
R. Mangles, Esq.
Fitzherbert Macdonald, Esq.
William Morgan, Esq. (5 copies).
F. Mead, Esq.
E. Meade, Esq.
Captain R. Morgan, R.N.
Captain McDonald.
Vincent Mackesy, Esq., 63rd Regiment.
Colonel Martin, Royal Dragoons.
Lieut.-Colonel Maxwell, 82nd Regiment.
Officers' Library, 82nd Regiment.
Captain Marriott, 82nd Regiment.
Lieut.-Colonel Willoughby Moore, 6th Dragoons.
Lieutenant R. G. Manley, 6th Dragoons.
R. Maule, Esq., 82nd Regiment.
William Morris, Esq.
David Morris, Esq., M.P.
John Carnac Morris.
Major Mann, 90th Light Infantry, Major of Brigade, Carmarthen.
Colonel Eaton Monins.
Colonel Norcliffe, K.H.
Fletcher Norton, Esq.
Lieut.-Colonel Nepean.
H. F. Oldfield, Esq.
Major Oldfield.
Mrs. Parks.
William Prinsep, Esq.

LIST OF SUBSCRIBERS.

xxiii

R. Prescott, Esq.
Major Pattle, 16th Lancers.
Lieut.-Colonel Pratt.
Captain Robert Peel, 6th Dragoons.
Captain Probyn, 6th Dragoons.
Captain Pardoe, 82nd Regiment.
S. W. Penn, Esq., Royal Artillery.
The Rev. R. Purvis.
Major Parkinson, A.D.C. to Major-General Love.
Mrs. Rennell.
Dr. Robertson, M.D.
Colonel Ridley, Grenadier Guards.
Captain Roebuck.
Royal Military College.
Major-General Simpson, Commanding Depôt, Chatham.
Captain Sterling, R.N.
Thomas Smallpage, Esq.
Lieut.-Colonel Smyth, C.B., 16th Lancers.
Lieut.-Colonel Staunton, 31st Regiment.
Lieut.-Colonel Sullivan, A. A. General, Horse Guards.
F. Say, Esq.
H. Starkie, Esq.
Lieutenant Miles Stringer, 6th Dragoons.
Herbert Taylor, Esq.
Rev. William Thursby.
Colonel Tomkinson.
Richard Thompson, Esq.
J. H. Thursby, Esq.
Lieutenant Harry R. S. Trelawny, 6th Dragoons.
Lieut.-Colonel Robert Vandeleur.
H. Walpole Vade, Esq.
Colonel Lloyd Vaughan Watkins, M.P., Lord Lieutenant of Brecknockshire.
Lieut.-Colonel Wells, C.B.
Mrs. Wells.
Joshua Walker, Esq.
Major R. Weyland.
Major White.

Charles Baring Wall, Esq., M.P., F.R.S., F.S.A.
Lieutenant Bigoe Williams, Esq., 4th Dragoon Guards.
Major Henry White, 6th Dragoons.
Lieut.-Colonel Williams, 2nd Life Guards.
Lieutenant H. Walters, 6th Dragoons.
Dr. Woodham, Jesus College, Cambridge.
Dr. Winter, St. John's College, Oxford.
Dr. Winter, for St. John's College Library.
B. Eveleigh Winthrop, Esq.

ERRATUM.

Page 140, line 11, *for* " one square," *read* one squad.

HISTORY

OF THE

DRESS OF THE BRITISH SOLDIER.

ANCIENT BRITISH PERIOD.

B.C. 55.

FIFTY-FIVE years before the birth of Christ, Julius Cæsar landed on the shores of Britain, and found the inhabitants of Cantium (Kent) the most civilized of all the Britons, and differing but little in their manners from the Gauls, from whom they had most probably acquired the arts of spinning, dyeing, and weaving wool. There is much obscurity about their dress, therefore a drawing is not attempted. Sir Richard Hoare says that the ordinary dress of the early Britons was the skin of a brindled or spotted cow, or made of the skins of the beasts killed in hunting, or a cloak of sheepskin; and that, before the Roman invasion, the dress of the chieftains consisted of a close coat, or covering for the body, called by Dio a tunic, and described as chequered with various colours in divisions. Below were loose pantaloons, called by the Irish *brigis*, and by the Romans *bragis* and *bracæ*, whence the modern term *breeches*; on the head a conical cap, called *cab*; shoes made of raw hide, the hair turned outwards. Various accounts state that the warriors punctured and painted their bodies with a colour made from the herb called glastum or woad, which was of a blue colour; Cæsar says, to make them look dreadful in battle. The Romans, on their first invasion, imagined that they lived constantly in "*puris naturalibus*," because they stripped themselves nearly naked to be free for the encounter. We have, however, the testimony of Cæsar to the fact, that even the least civilized were clad in skins, and the southern Britons, like the Gauls, were frequently splendidly attired. Men of rank amongst the Gauls and Britons, according to Cæsar and Diodorus, shaved the chin, but wore immense tangled moustaches, some of them hanging down on their breasts. Over the tunic, both Gauls and Britons wore the *sagum*, a short cloak so called by the Romans. The British *sagum* was of one uniform colour, generally either blue or black.

The arms of the ancient British were the lance, or spear, the sword, dagger, bows and arrows, and the battle-axe. The metal used in their construction was bronze. Their shields were flat and circular, made of wicker, likewise their quivers; and many of them were covered with metal. Several brazen swords and spear-heads were found in the bed of the river Thames, near Kingston, and many have been found in other places. The usual method of their fighting is said to have been on horseback and in chariots. It is probable that the inhabitants of Gaul and Britain were originally the same people; they had the same customs, their language, arms, names of towns and persons, were similar, and both descended from the Scythians.

THE ROMAN BRITISH PERIOD.

A.D. 78—400.

It would have been surprising if a civilized people like the Romans, who conquered and held possession of Britain for upwards of 300 years, had not introduced many of their customs into the country: it appears that before the close of the first century, their dress was in some measure adopted by the inhabitants. " The sons of the British chieftains," says Tacitus, " began to affect our dress:" the *bracæ* were abandoned by the southern and eastern Britons; and the Roman tunic, reaching nearly to the knee, with the cloak or mantle—still, however, called the *sagum*— became the general habit of the better class. The pre-eminent dress of the Romans, and which distinguished them in a marked way from the

I.

A.D. 78-400.

Greeks, as well as from the barbarians, was the toga, which appears to have remained the costume of the state with the patricians until the last days of Roman splendour; and it may be asserted, that not until the empire was transferred to Constantinople, did the toga become entirely superseded by that more decidedly Grecian dress, the *pallium*. There are considerable doubts as to the true form of the toga. The tunic was a later introduction among the Romans than the toga, which reached more than half way down the thigh. Soldiers, when in camp, wore the tunic without the toga. The pallium, or mantle, being less cumbersome and trailing than the toga, superseded the latter. When worn over armour, and fastened on the right shoulder with a clasp or button, this cloak was called *paludamentum*.

The costume of the Roman soldiers, who played so conspicuous a part at this period in Britain, may be obtained in all its varieties, by a reference to the famous work of Montfaucon (*Antiquité Expliquée*).

The two soldiers drawn in Plate I. may be considered to be a fair representation of the foot soldier of the Roman legions. The first wears a cuirass of scale armour, formed of flexible plates of steel on a substructure of leather, lapping over each other, and allowing full play to the motion of the body. The other figure wears the laminated cuirass, consisting of bands of brass about three inches wide, wrapping half round the body, and fastened on a leather or quilted substructure; the shoulders being also covered with similar bands. They both wear tunics reaching nearly to the knees, and the drawers appear as low as the calf of the leg. The military sandals, which vary in shape, were called *caligæ;* they were set with nails underneath, to prevent slipping. A short sword, for either cutting or thrusting, having the blade edged on both sides. The shields here represented are of two kinds; and there were others of different shapes. The Roman cavalry, after the conquest of Greece, were armed much like the infantry, carrying swords, shields, and javelins, with points at both ends. Complete Roman armour consisted of the helmet, shield, lorica, and greaves. The lorica was originally of leather, but in the time of Severus (according to Livy) the whole of the Roman armour was of brass.

ANGLO-SAXON PERIOD.

A.D. 450—1016.

A WELSH bard, by name Anuerin, who flourished early in the sixth century, and who fought in person against the invaders of his country, gives the following account, in his famous poem, called "Gododen," of the battle of Cattraeth: "There were present," he writes, "three hundred warriors, arrayed in gilded armour; three loricated bands, with three commanders wearing golden torques; they were armed with daggers, white sheathed piercers, and wore four pointed (square) helmets; some of them carried spears and shields, the latter being made of split wood. Their leader had a projecting shield: he was harnessed in scaly mail, armed with a slaughtering pike, and wore the skin of a beast." The scaly mail of which Anuerin speaks, was the well-known armour of the Sarmatian and Gothic tribes, from whence the Romans derived their *lorica squamata*. Mael was, indeed, but the British word for iron; the tunic covered with rings, to which the word mail was afterwards applied by the Norman French, was literally called by the Saxons *gehrynged byrn*, ringed armour. The square, or four pointed helmet, was worn as late as the ninth century in France, by the guards of Lothaire and Charles the Bald: and square crowns are sometimes seen in the Anglo-Saxon illuminations. In a MS. in the Cotton collection, marked "Claudius, B. 4," there is one of the earliest specimens of the ringed *byrn*, borrowed from the Phrygians, which was formed of rings sewn flat upon a leather tunic. In the year 1779, an ancient barrow was opened near Chatham, a skeleton was found within, with an iron spear-head fifteen inches long, an iron knife, an iron sword thirty-five and a quarter inches long from the point to the bottom of the handle, which was all in one piece; the blade was thirty inches long, two in breadth, flat, double-edged, and sharp pointed: it is supposed these were the arms of the Anglo-Saxons.

It is recorded of the Danes, that when established in England, and on their conversion to Christianity, they cast off the former colour of their dress, which used to be black, and adopted gay colours, and endeavoured to outshine the Saxon; for it is said, "the Danes were effeminately gay in their dress, combed their hair once a day, bathed once a week, and often changed their attire: by these means they pleased the eyes of women." Saxon military and civil costume differed but little. Many warriors are represented with no other weapon but a shield and a spear, axe, or bow and arrows, and without any addition to their ordinary dress; but, in fact, they were all soldiers, the addition of a spear, a shield, and sometimes but not invariably a helmet made them ready for the fray. The sword was almost generally worn, indeed there was a severe penance in the ancient canons for going unarmed. The short linen tunic was preferred to all other vestments, as the one in which they could the most freely wield their weapons; and the only addition to that commonly worn, was a metal collar which acted as a breastplate, and was called *bræst-beden* or *bræst-beorg*, breast defence or breast guard. Although this continued to be their general habit in war, they were not unacquainted with defensive body armour, for as early as the eighth century they were familiar with the tunic of rings, called byrn. The cap was of the Phrygian shape, apparently made of leather, sometimes bound and bordered with metal. The leather helme is frequently mentioned by Saxon writers, as is also the felten hat, the felt or woollen hat, —a cap completely conical and without ornament, occurs in some MSS., and appears from its shape the immediate predecessor of the nasal helmet of the eleventh century. The shields varied in size; they were oval and convex, and some nearly large enough to cover the whole figure; they were generally painted with a white ground and of various colours in circles: some were gilt. The sword was two-edged, long and straight. Their weapons were all formed of iron, and consisted of long broadswords double-edged, daggers, javelins, and long spears, some of which were barbed and others broad and leaf-shaped. The spear-head seems to have been variously formed; and they used the byl, which is stated to have been very destructive at the battle of Hastings; and the battle-axe was also used with great success; it broke in pieces coats of mail, and the steel casques of the Normans: their large shields protected them from the arrows, and they stood firm against William's horse; surrender was a word unknown to them. The ringed armour alluded to, consisted of a tunic, perhaps made of quilted cloth or leather, upon which was fastened rings of iron, side by side, covering the entire surface, similar to some of those worn by the soldiers of William the Conqueror. It is curious to remark, that so far back as Harold the Second, there were complaints that the English took their fashions from the French. The monkish chroniclers declare, that the English had transformed themselves in speech and garb, and adopted all that was ridiculous in the manners of these people for their own; they shortened their tunics, they trimmed their hair, they loaded their arms with golden bracelets, and entirely forgot their usual simplicity. In the military habit Harold ordered a change, which led to a decisive success in Wales. The heavy armour of the Saxon (for the tunic covered with rings was considerable in weight) rendered them unable to pursue the Welsh to their recesses. Harold observed this impediment, and commanded them to use armour made of leather only, and lighter weapons. This leather armour consisted in overlapping flaps, cut into the shape of scales or leaves, called *corium*, or in the Norman laws *corietum*.

Plate II. represents two Anglo-Saxons, one with a coat of rings, a large shield, and a simple conical cap; the other in a tunic without mail, a small shield, and a Phrygian cap.

In the beginning of the seventh century the British chiefs were in the habit of wearing skin kilts (striped kilts were common); and as the inhabitants of North Britain were on intimate terms with their neighbours, it is highly probable that the Scottish kilt is much older than generally supposed.

II

A D 400-1016

III.

A.D. 1066–1087.

THE NORMANS.

A.D. 1066—1087.

THE military habit of this period has several novelties: the first is the capuchon or cowl to the tunic, covered with rings, which does not appear in Saxon illuminations; over this is placed a conical helmet, with its nasal, and, in some instances, with a neck-piece behind. Both Normans and Saxons are represented in the tunic reaching nearly to the knee, and being cut up behind and before for general convenience. In the rudeness of some of the representations it appears as though it terminated in short trousers. The Norman name for this military vestment was hauberk. The best pictorial authority for the dress of the Norman soldier, at the time of the conquest of England, is that curious relic, the Bayeux tapestry; but the work was originally rude, and time has much defaced it, so that it is difficult correctly to understand what may have been intended to be represented.

Besides the hauberk of rings, there are some marked with transverse lines, so as to give the idea of either being quilted, or stitched in chequers, or covered with small lozenge-shaped pieces of steel instead of rings, known about this period by the name of mascled armour, from its resemblance to the meshes of a net. Other descriptions of armour were in use, and in some instances the hauberks appear to be composed of rings and mascles mixed; in others, the body is diamonded, and the cowl and arms covered with rings.

The archers were a most important arm of the troops, who did the Conqueror invaluable service at Hastings, and made the bow for many centuries the chief strength of the English lines.

Plate III. represents three Norman soldiers, one of them an archer, with a close vest covered with rings, wide breeches gathered above and below the knee, and ornamented with two large red spots. The other soldier on foot has a tunic divided with small squares, and rings in the middle of them; he has a kite-shaped shield, with a nondescript dragon on it, a byl or war-hatchet in his hand, and a conical cap on his head, with a nasal to it. The mounted soldier has mascled armour, and is armed with a gonfanon. The peculiar fashion of shaving the back of the head is shown.

The military tunic called hauberk, which was, it is stated, of German origin, Meyrick says, " probably so entitled from *haven*, to hew or cut, and *berg*, a defence, that is, a defence against cuts or stabs; the sleeves and skirts of the hauberk had yellow borders, whether of metal for defence, or of gilt for ornament, cannot now be decided." The Norman shields were nearly of the shape of a boy's kite of the present day; they had, besides the straps called holders through which the arm passed, a long slip of leather which went round the neck, and was an additional support, enabling both hands to be used with greater facility; this strap was called *guige;* it gave the Norman great advantage over the Anglo-Saxon, who held his shield at arm's length with a clenched hand, consequently could not use the two-handed sword, which the Norman did with much effect. The shields were ornamented with fantastic devices, such as griffins, dragons, &c. &c., but without heraldic bearings. Their arms were the sword, the axe, the spear, and bows and arrows. The spear was sometimes ornamented with a small flag fixed just below the metal point, and termed, in the language of that day, *gonfanon,* or *gonfalon.* Upwards of 700 years have elapsed since the Conquest; the gonfanon has again become an English military weapon for cavalry, called a lance. The axe continued in use long after this period; Stephen fought with it at the siege of Lincoln, in 1141, until it snapped within his grasp. Archers were both mounted and on foot. The Saxons had neglected, or totally discontinued them. Henry of Huntingdon makes William speak of the Saxons as a nation not even having arrows. To the arrows of the Normans at the battle of Hastings is attributed the issue of that contest; a random shaft, it is well known, struck Harold in the eye and slew him. The battle-axes and byls of the Saxon infantry are recorded to have made terrible havoc amongst the Normans. There was a striking peculiarity in the Normans who came with William; they not only shaved the face entirely, in contra-

IIII.

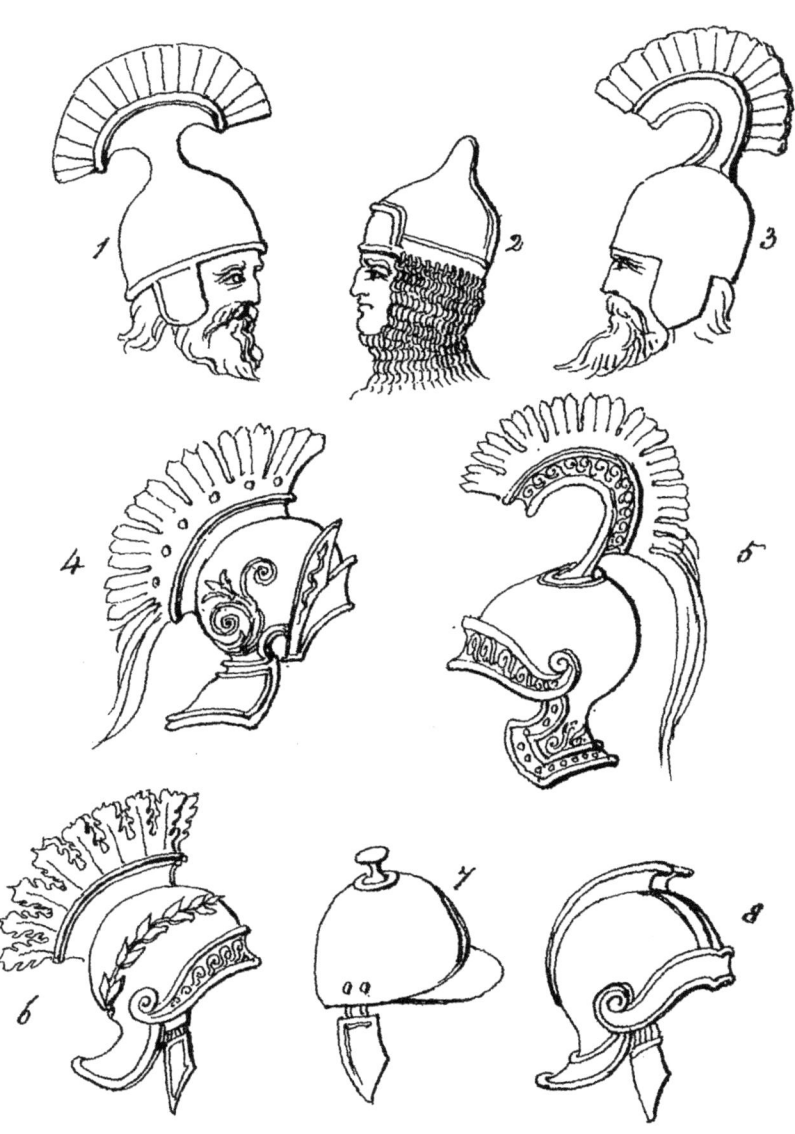

B.C. 870–A.D. 1400

distinction to the Anglo-Saxons, who left at least the upper lip unshorn, but they shaved the back of the head; it was so great a novelty that the spies sent by Harold to reconnoitre the camp of William, declared they had seen no soldiers, but an army of priests. This fashion is supposed to have been adopted from the nobles of Aquitaine, who had been distinguished by so extraordinary a practice for many years previous to the Conquest.

Fashion has ever been blindly submitted to: scarcely any thing has been too ridiculous or too useless to prevent its being followed.

In Plate IV. eight helmets are portrayed, to show that from the earliest period helmets have been worn, with ornaments on the top of them, similar to those of modern times; ornaments not only useless, but exceedingly inconvenient, by adding a top weight to the cap, which, for military purposes, and for the comfort of the wearer, should sit as firmly on the head as it is possible to make it. Nos. 1, 2, and 3, are Assyrian helmets, of a date 870 years before Christ. No. 2, is a serviceable one. Nos. 1 and 3 are preposterous: nevertheless, helmets very similar in shape were adopted by the Grecians (shown in Nos. 4 and 5); and the Romans at one period run into the same absurd practice. No. 6 is a specimen. No. 8 is the Roman helmet worn during the republic; well calculated for its purpose. No. 7 is a Roman British helmet, found in Hertfordshire, made of bronze. The Assyrian helmets, mentioned above, are taken from drawings in Layard's Nineveh.

REIGNS OF WILLIAM II., HENRY I., AND STEPHEN.

A.D. 1087—1154.

The Normans and Flemings who accompanied the Conqueror to England, and those who followed him in great numbers afterwards, are said by our early historians to have been remarkable for their ostentation and love of finery: personal decoration was their chief study, and new fashions were continually introduced by them. Peaked-toed shoes and boots, of an absurd shape, excited the wrath of the monkish historians. Ordericus Vibalis says they were invented by some one deformed in the foot. Peaked-toed boots were strictly forbidden to the clergy. The shoes, called *pigaciæ*, had their points made like a scorpion's tail: and a courtier, named Robert, stuffed his out with tow, and caused them to curl round like a ram's horn—a fashion which took mightily amongst the nobles. The custom of shaving the back of the head, amongst the Normans, has been noticed. On their establishment in England, this unbecoming custom was abandoned; and with the usual caprice of fashion, they ran into the opposite extreme. William of Malmsbury, who lamented over the cropping system, during the reign of Rufus, reprobated the long hair, the loose flowing garments, the extravagantly pointed shoes, and the unweaponed effeminate appearance of the youths of that day. In 1104, when Henry I. was in Normandy, a prelate, named Serlo, preached against the fashion of wearing long hair so eloquently, that the monarch and his courtiers were moved to tears; and taking advantage of the impression he had produced, the enthusiastic prelate whipped a pair of scissors out of his sleeves, and cropped the whole congregation! This was followed by a royal edict, prohibiting the wearing of long hair; but in the next reign, that of Stephen, the old fashion was revived; when in 1139, it received a sudden check from a trifling circumstance. A young soldier, whose chief pride lay in the beauty of his locks, which hung down almost to his knees, dreamed one night that a man strangled him with his own ringlets: the dream had such an effect upon him that he immediately cut them off, and cropping became again the order of the day. But this reformation, adds the historian, did not last long; scarcely a year elapsed before the people returned to their former follies; and those who wished to be thought courtiers, permitted their hair to grow to such a shameful length that they resembled women: those who had not abundance of hair wore wigs; and from this date they may be said to have been invented. Perruquiers ought, therefore, to assume three Sagittarii for their arms, in honour of King Stephen. The armour and weapons of the time of the Conquest continued, with little variation, to the close of the twelfth century. William Rufus (1087—1100) is represented on his great seal in a scaly suit of steel or leather armour, with, in lieu of a nasal helmet, a new head piece, called by the Normans a *chapelle-de-fer*—an iron cap, of a very Tartar-like shape. Henry I. (1100—1135), on his great seal, wears a hauberk of flat rings; and the seal of Milo Fitzwalter, constable of England, and governor of Gloucester, during his reign, exhibits the baron in a suit of mascled, or quilted armour, of the same shape as those in the Bayeux tapestry, with a gonfanon, a kite-shaped shield, and a chapelle-de-fer. Stephen (1135—1154) appears on his great seal in a hauberk of rings, set edgewise; an improvement upon the flat-ringed armour in point of security, though much heavier to the wearer. And the seal of Richard, constable of Chester, of the same period, represents a warrior, wearing a suit of what Sir S. Meyrick denominated *tegulated* armour, it being composed of small square plates of steel, lapping over each other like tiles. The nasal helmet, gonfanon, and kite-shaped shield, appear also on this seal; and the long pointed toes to the chausses, are curiously illustrative of the period. Thus we have evidence of five or six varieties of body armour during the first half of the twelfth century; besides which, there was what Sir S. Meyrick calls trellised or broigned, rusted and banded. The ingenuity both of armourers and warriors, was naturally in continued exertion to invent such defence for the body, as would be proof against all the rapidly invented weapons for the purposes of destruction: alterations were constantly taking place, but too minute for delineation then, or for distinction now, when time has half obliterated the details of objects, at first but imperfectly represented by the rude artists of this dark but interesting period. The hauberk, covered with flat rings, or with rings set upon their edges, and closely stitched together, which is denominated single mail, is the most obvious armour discernible from the close of the tenth century to the reign of Edward I., and that scales and mascles are the principal varieties. When Magnus Barefoot, King of Norway (1093—1103), led his forces to Britain, he was opposed, near the Isle of Anglesea, by two earls, Hugh the Proud, and Hugh the Fat. The king shot an arrow against the former, and at the same moment another arrow was launched in the same direction by one of his followers: the earl was so enveloped in mail, that no part was exposed except his eyes, and both arrows striking at once on the earl's face, one of them broke his nasal, whilst the other perforated the eye and brain, so that he immediately fell dead. The custom of hooking up the collar to the nasal was followed by the introduction of steel cheek-pieces, either pendant to the sides of the helmet, or worn beneath like a half mask, with apertures for the eyes. The Normans called all these defences for the face, *ventaille*, or *aventaille* (i. e. *avant-taille*), and the word being afterwards applied to the vizor, has occasioned many writers to confound things of which the use was the same, but the shape and material totally different. The spur remained a single goad, and the shield kite form, and without heraldic bearings. Stephen is said to have adopted the sign Sagittarius for his device, as already observed; but his shield is perfectly plain, and his gonfanon bears a simple cross: on his seal is a star or sun, and on that of Henry I. a flower.

REIGNS OF HENRY II., RICHARD I., AND JOHN.

A.D. 1154—1216.

THE earliest monumental effigy of an English sovereign is that of Henry II. in the abbey of Fontevraud, Normandy. The right hand, on which was the great ring, is broken, but contains a portion of the sceptre, which, to judge from certain marks on the breast of the figure, must have been remarkably short. The beard is painted and pencilled like a miniature, to represent its being closely shaven (the old Norman custom at this time returned to); the mantle is fastened by a fibula on the right shoulder of a deep reddish chocolate colour; the dalmatica, or long tunic, is crimson, starred or flowered with gold. The boots green, with gold spurs, fastened by red leathers. The gloves have jewels on the centre of the back of the hand, a mark of

V.

A.D. 1154-1216

royalty, or high ecclesiastical rank. The crown has been many years broken, and an injudicious attempt has been made to restore it with plaster of Paris. The effigy of Richard I. is in the same abbey—and this, as well as that of King John at Worcester, are attired much in the same way—both are represented with beards and moustaches, which came again into fashion towards the close of Richard's reign. The military habits during this reign underwent no distinguishable change, but there were novelties during the reign of Richard I. and John—the shield emblazoned with heraldic bearings; the long tunic worn under, and the surcoat worn over the coat of mail, usually made of silk of one uniform colour, but sometimes variegated, sometimes richly embroidered, and sometimes altogether of cloth of gold or silver. Both the seals of Richard I. represent him with a long tunic under the hauberk, and his brother John is in a surcoat.

It has been conjectured that the custom originated with the Crusaders, both for the purpose of distinguishing the many different leaders serving under the cross, and to veil the iron armour so apt to heat when exposed to the direct rays of the sun. The date of its first appearance in Europe, and the circumstances of the Knights of St. John and of the Temple being so attired in their monumental effigies, are certainly arguments in favour of the supposition. The drawings of two knights of the time of Henry II., delineated in Plate V., are taken from monumental effigies of this period.

The representation of Crusaders in Plate VI. is also of this date The third crusade of Richard I. was in 1190, 1191. He was detained by Leopold, Duke of Austria, and sold to the Emperor Henry VI., on his return to England, after defeating Saladin at Jaffa. It is not surprising that the Crusaders should have lost so many men and horses, loaded as they were with armour of the heaviest description. Besides the surcoat, two other military garments are common to this period, the *wambegs* or *gambeson*, and the *haqueton* or *aiketon;* they were wadded and quilted tunics, the first according to Sir S. Merrick, of leather stuffed with wool, and the second of buckskin filled with cotton; these were worn by those who could not afford hauberks. The helmet towards the close of the twelfth century had assumed the shape of a sugar-loaf, but suddenly during the reign of Richard I. it lost its lofty cone, and subsided into a flat-topped steel cap, with a hoop of iron passing under the chin, the face being protected by a movable grating affixed to a hinge on one side, and fastened by a pin on the other, so that it opened like a wicket, and might be taken off or put on as occasion required. This was called the *aventaille* or *ventail*, as the earlier defences for the face had been before.

The *plastron de fer* or steel-plate, introduced during this century to prevent the pressure of the hauberk upon the chest, was sometimes worn under the gambeson, sometimes between it and the hauberk. In a combat between Richard Cœur de Lion, then Earl of Poitou, and a knight named William de Barris, they charged each other so furiously, that their lances pierced through their shields, hauberks, and gambesons, and were only prevented by their plastrons from transfixing their bodies. In later times the plastron is called the gorget. The shields in the reigns of Richard I. and John decreased in length, and became less arched at the top; they were afterwards called heater-shaped. To the spear, sword, battle-axe, and bow, we have to add the arbaliste or crossbow, introduced during the reign of Richard I., who was killed by a shaft from that weapon. It continued in use till musketry superseded it. A very ancient weapon called *gisarme, guisarme, gysarme, juisarme*, is not very well described by any writer; it seems to have been a weapon formed with a lance and a hook on one side of it, both to unhorse the rider and wound him also, and to leave him exposed to attack by swords.

A remarkable occurrence took place in this reign. The Bishop of Norwich, for divers military offences as a general officer, appeared before a tribunal, and was punished with the seizure of his temporalities and a considerable fine.

There was a curious law enacted during the reign of Richard I. for the government of those going by sea to the Holy Land :—" He who

VI.

A D 1154-1242.

kills a man on shipboard, shall be bound to the dead body and thrown into the sea; if the man is killed on shore, the slayer shall be bound to the dead body and buried with it. He who shall draw his knife to strike another, or who shall have drawn blood from him, to lose his hand; if he shall have only struck with the palm of his hand without drawing blood, he shall be thrice ducked in the sea," &c. &c.

Description of PLATE VII.

No. 1 represents mail of a very early period, and seems to have been used by the Normans. It consists of small iron rings sewn on a substratum of leather.

No. 2 is another kind of mail, with the rings set edgeways.

No. 3 is rather imaginary, but it looks like the dress of the Norman soldiers as represented in the Bayeux tapestry, which seems to be made of a substructure of leather, with small squares made by sewing small pieces of metal to it, and within the squares rings.

No. 5. is the mail which is made by small rings uniting each other, and without any substructure. This varied a good deal in the size of the rings, some being made of larger and others of smaller. No. 4 is the same mail, only the rings are drawn much closer together; and No. 6 is the way in which it is made, one ring uniting four others.

No. 7 is the fragment of a curious portral or breast-guard of a horse, which is in the Tower. It is formed of small round pieces of metal, about the size of a penny-piece, and is called penny-plate armour. It is probably not of earlier date than Henry VII.

VII

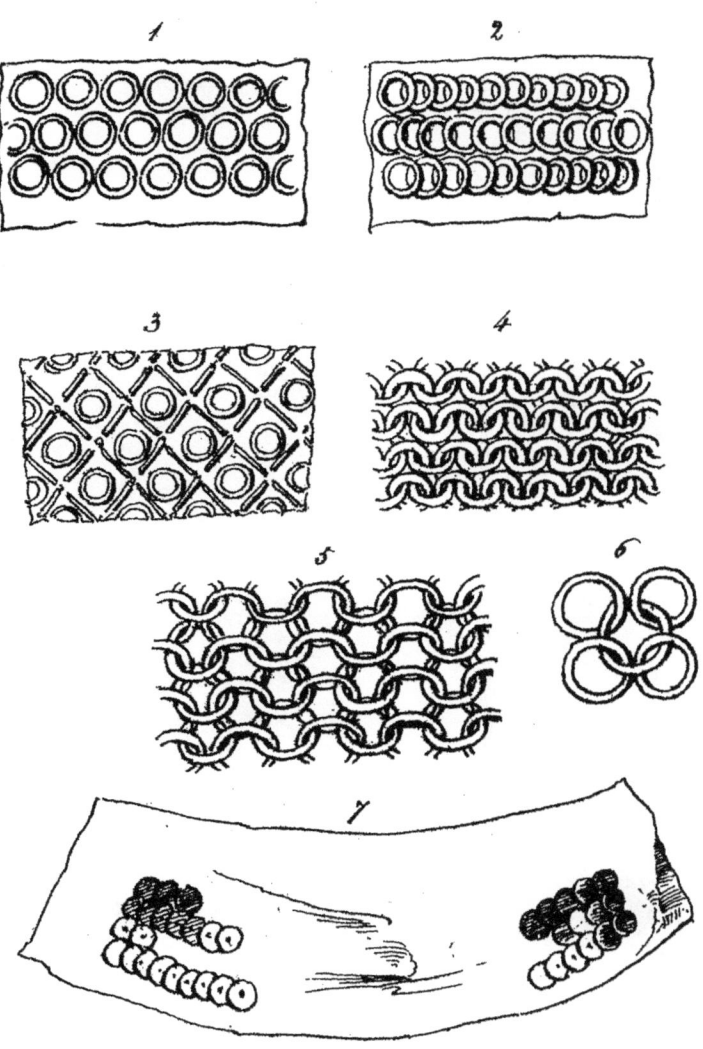

A. D. 450-1399.

HENRY III.

A.D. 1216—1272.

The long reign of Henry III. embraces the greater part of the thirteenth century, but its costume is more remarkable for increase of splendour than for alteration of form. Matthew Paris, the monk of St. Alban's, a faithful historian, and an eye-witness of much of the pageantry he describes, represents himself disgusted rather than pleased by the excessive foppery of the times.

The military habit underwent several changes: quilted and padded armour of silk, cloth, buckram, or leather, came still more into use; and, from the peculiar work with which it was now ornamented, obtained the name of *pourpoint*, and *counterpoint*: a complete suit, consisting of a sleeved tunic and chausses, was frequently worn by the knights of this period beneath the surcoat, which was considerably lengthened, and, during this reign, first emblazoned with the arms of the wearer. The flat-ringed armour nearly disappeared, and that composed of rings set up edgeways seems to have been the most generally worn mail of the thirteenth century. But during this reign a new species was introduced from Asia, where it is still worn. This consisted of four rings connected by a fifth, all of which were so fastened with rivets, that they formed a complete garment of themselves without any foundation,—see No. V., Plate 7. There were other changes which took place during the reign of Henry III. The flat-topped cylindrical helmet of the reigns of Richard and John descended no lower than the ears, the face being covered by the aventaille, but in this reign it covered the whole head and rested on the shoulders, and by degrees assumed a barrel form bulging at the sides. These great helmets were only worn when in positive action, being too heavy and cumbrous for general use, and when forcibly turned round upon the shoulders by a vigorous stroke of a lance, severely hurt the wearer. In the romance of Lancelot du Lac, the helmet of a knight is said to have been so turned, that the edges grazed his shoulders, and "ses armes étoient toutes ensanglantées;" apertures for the sight and breathing were cut in them in the shape of a cross, to which was added sometimes a cluster of simple perforations. The martel de fer (a pointed hammer, or a small pickaxe,) was added to the offensive weapons, making sad havoc with the various species of mail, breaking the links of chain and picking off the scales and plates, leaving fatal openings for the passage of the sword and the lance.

The archers of this reign are represented in ringed hauberks, with sleeves to the elbow, over which appear vests of leather, defended by four circular iron plates.

The rowelled spur is first seen on the great seal of Henry III.; but it is not common before the reign of Edward I.

Plate VIII.

Nos. 1 and 3 are Anglo-Saxon helmets, probably made of leather. No. 3 is ornamented with a metal binding and brass studs.

No. 2 is a drawing of one of the oldest pieces of armour hanging up in the Tower; it is dated Edward II., reign 1307.

No. 4 is an early British helmet found in Cardiganshire.

No. 5. A curious head-dress, called Edward the Confessor's crown.

Nos. 6 and 7 are of the time of Henry III., from 1154 to 1216.

No. 8. A helmet of the time of Richard I., 1189.

VIII.

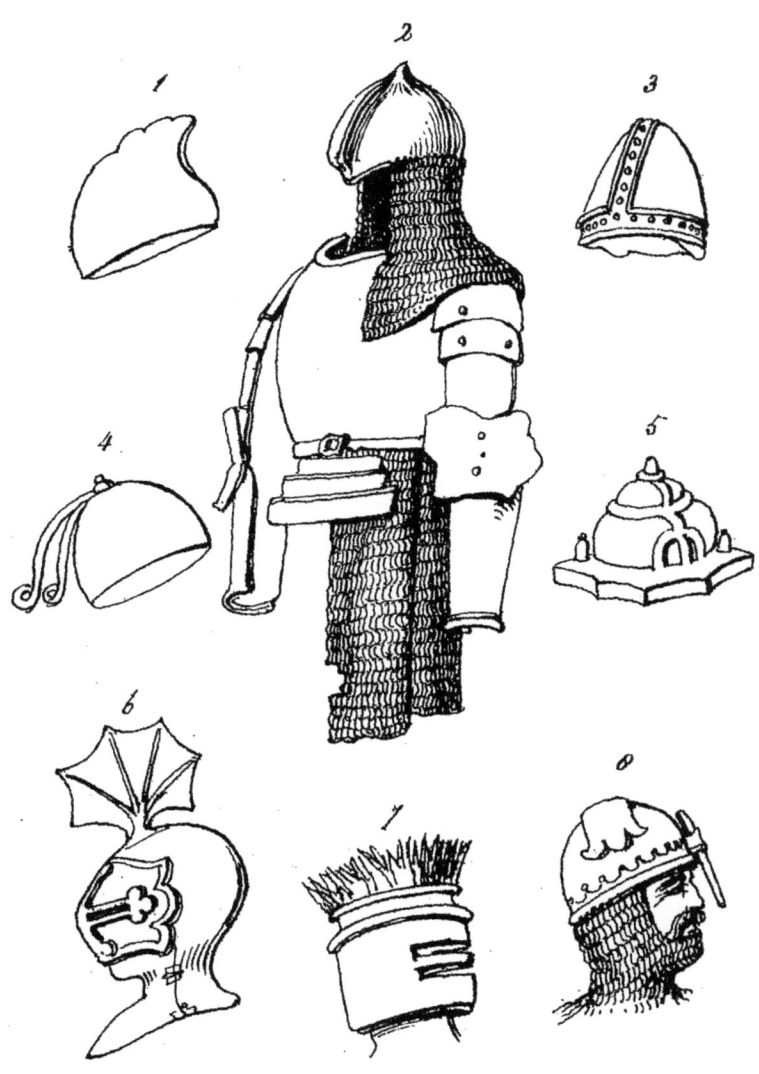

A.D. 450.—1399.

EDWARD I.

A.D. 1272—1307.

EDWARD I. was as simple in his dress as he was magnificent in his liberalities. He never wore his crown after the day of his coronation, and preferred to the royal garments of purple, the common dress of a citizen. Being asked one day why he did not wear richer clothing, he answered that it was absurd to suppose that he was more estimable in fine than in simple apparel. The emblazoned surcoat came into more general usage in this reign. The *cyclas*, the *bliaus*, and the *contise*, all worn over the shirt of mail, as well as over the more peaceful tunic, were richly embroidered, either with fanciful devices or the armorial bearings of the owner. Towards the close of this reign those curious ornaments, called *ailettes*, or little wings, from their situation and appearance, are seen on the shoulders of knights either in battle or in the lists, but they did not become general till the next reign. The helmet is frequently mounted by the heraldic crest, and this picturesque but inconvenient decoration became henceforward a principal feature of the chivalric equipment. The top of the helmet inclines to a cone in some instances; and the front, seen in profile, presents almost an angular appearance. Skullcaps or chapels-de-fer, both spherical and conical, the latter the prototype of the bascinet, and indeed already so called, were worn over the mail-coif, and commonly with the nasal, which disappears after this reign. Leathern gauntlets appear reaching higher than the wrist, but not yet plated. The shield is sometimes flat, and nearly triangular or heater-shaped; others are pear-shaped and semi-cylindrical. The lance has lost its gonfanon; and the *pennon*, which resembles it in its swallow-tailed form, but longer and broader, becomes a military ensign, and is generally charged with the crest, badge, or war-cry of the knight; his arms being emblazoned on the banner, which is in shape a parallelogram. Edward I. had banners emblazoned with the arms of England, gules, three lions passant regardant; of St. George, argent, a cross gules; of

St. Edmund, azure, three crowns or; and of St. Edward the Confessor, azure, a cross fleury between six martlets or.

The *falchion*, a peculiarly shaped broad-bladed sword; the *estoc*, a small stabbing sword; the *anelace* or *anelas*, a broad dagger, tapering to a very fine point; and the *coutel* or *cuttelas* (whence cutlass), a military knife, are added to the offensive weapons.

The mace also first appears in illuminations, though it may have been introduced during the earlier crusades, as it is evidently of oriental origin.

EDWARD II.

A.D. 1307—1327.

THE twenty troublesome years of the reign of Edward II. were remarkable for the increase of luxury in proportion to the decline of honour and virtue. Excited by the example of the profligate and presumptuous Gaveston, "the esquire endeavoured to outshine the knight, the knight the baron, the baron the earl, and the earl the king himself in the richness of his apparel." Beards were worn apparently by persons in years, great officers of state, and knights templars, but not generally. The military habit of this period is generally recognised by a greater admixture of plate with the chain. The hauberk and chausses are now nearly covered with wrought iron.

Brasserts connect the shoulder with the elbow pieces, and avant-bras or vant-braces defend the arm from the latter to the wrist. Greaves of one plate protect the fore part of the leg, and on the breast are fastened sometimes one, sometimes two round plates, called *mamelieres*, from their position, to which are appended chains attached at the other end, one to the sword hilt, and the other to the helmet, which, at the moment of action, was placed over the *coif de mailles* or the *bascinet*, which latter appears in this reign in a more important shape, without the nasal, and occasionally with a movable visor, which renders the helmet unneces-

IX.

A D 1372—1377

sary. The flat-topped, barrel-shaped helmet seems to have been abandoned about this time; and that important piece of armour, which at the close of Edward the First's reign had been tending towards the conical, now assumed the sugar-loaf or egg-like form. The conical-topped helmet with the angular projection in front, outlived the new fashion, as we shall find in the next reign. The *ailettes* were very generally worn, and a neck guard of chain was added to the bascinet and called the *camail*, either corrupted from *cap-mail*, or from resembling the lower part of the capuchon, commonly worn by all classes, but which among the higher ranks was made of camels' hair, and therefore termed *camelin* by the French, and camelotum by the Latin writers, from whence our word camlet, afterwards applied to an inferior stuff made in imitation of it. The cyclas, or surcoat, is sometimes considerably shorter in front than behind (see Plate IX.). The figure on the left of the print represents a knight of the reign of Edward I., with a *nasal* to his helmet, mamelieres, and ailettes; the knight on the right is in the armour of the time of Edward II.; and the one in the centre is of the period of Edward the Third's reign, very much changed in character, the armour being formed mostly of plates. The archers in this reign were nearly in a uniform costume, mounted and on foot, and cross-bow men. They wore hauberks and chausses of gamboised work, with surcoats over them, and conical helmets with visors affixed, made of a perforated plate; they were made fast to the head by something like platted ropes. Bruce, at the battle of Bannockburn in 1313, dismounted all his horse, and formed his forces, with an army of foot, about 40,000 men: each man wore light armour which a sword could not easily pierce, battle-axes were at their sides, and lances in their hands. An inferior kind of cavalry in this reign were called hobilers; they were bound to keep a little nag for the purpose of giving notice of invasion; they were stationed at Portsmouth and other maritime places; they had a hacketon or armour of plates, a bascinet, iron gauntlets, a sword, knife, and a lance. To the offensive weapons were added, about this time, the scimiter, borrowed from the Turks, and a sort of poleaxe, called the *godenda* or *godendæ*. The *falcastrum*, a kind of bill or *gisarme*, was recommended for sea-fights; it is described as a scythe firmly fixed to a very long pole.

EDWARD III.

A.D. 1327—1377.

The reign of Edward III. is an important era in the history of costume. The complete changes that took place in every habit, civil or military, render its effigies and illuminations more distinctly conspicuous than those, perhaps, of any other age. The frequent tournaments and pageants of this period contributed to promote the succession of new fashions. The knights who attended them from all parts of Europe, were usually decorated with some quaint device suggested by gallantry, and endeavoured to outstrip each other in brilliancy of appearance. Armour became very splendid, so much so, say the old chroniclers, that the knights, who would otherwise have been taken prisoners, were frequently killed for the sake of their spoils. Many foreign fashions were introduced by the foreign knights; "the Englishmen, haunted so much unto the folly of strangers," says Dowglas, the monk of Glastonbury, "that every year they changed them in diverse shapes and disguisings of clothing; now long, now large, now strait, and every day clothingges new and destitute, and devest from all honesty of old arraye or good usage; and another time to short clothes and so straight-waisted, with full sleeves and tapetes (tippets), of surcoats and hodes, ouer long and large, all so nagged (gagged) and knib on euery side, and all so shattered, and also buttoned, that I with truth shall say, they seem more like the tormentors or devils in their clothing, and also in their shoying (shoeing) and other array, than they seemed to be like men."—(MS. Harleian Collect.)

In the thirty-seventh year of this reign, A.D. 1363, the Commons exhibited a complaint in Parliament against the general usage of expensive apparel, not suited either to the degree or income of the people; and an act was passed accordingly, restricting persons of certain ranks to certain clothing. The military habits present several striking novelties: the improved visored bascinet and camail, worn always for war, the crested helmet being reserved for the lists;

the magnificent jupon, emblazoned with the wearer's arms, or richly and fancifully embroidered; its constant and sumptuous companion, the military belt; the casing the body so nearly in complete steel, that plate armour may be said to commence from this period (see the centre knight in Plate IX.). The earliest military effigies of this reign still exhibit the cyclas shorter in front than behind, or the surcoat with indented borders. The principal causes of the adoption of plate armour were, according to Sir S. Meyrick, the excessive weight of chain mail, with its accompanying garments; indeed, it was so great that the knights sometimes sunk under it, suffocated with the heat as well as the burthen. The new steel back and breastplate enabled the wearer to dispense with the hauberk and the plastron, and the jupon was a much lighter and less cumbrous garment than either the surcoat or cyclas; besides, if of well-tempered metal, the plate could not be pierced or pushed into the body of the knight, as the hauberk was apt to be, if the gambeson or hacketon was imperfect underneath; the breast only at that time having the additional protection of a steel plate. The backs of the leathern gauntlets were furnished with overlapping plates, and the knuckles armed with knobs or spikes of iron, called *gads* or *gadlings*, the tops from the wrist being of steel, and lined with velvet. In a trial by combat adjudged between John de Visconté and Sir Thomas de la Marche, fought before Edward III. in close lists, at Westminster, Sir Thomas de la Marche gained the advantage by striking the gadlings of his gauntlets into the face of his adversary. The gauntlets of Edward the Black Prince are of brass or laton, and the gadlings, instead of being spikes, are made in the shape of lions or leopards. They hang above his tomb in Canterbury cathedral, with his velvet surcoat, which is gamboised and emblazoned with the arms of France and England, quarterly. The story of Edward being called the Black Prince from the colour of his armour seems to be exploded, and why he was so called is a matter of dispute and uncertainty. In the twenty-second year of this reign was founded the most noble order of the Garter—the circumstance that suggested the choice of this symbol is as great a mystery as the origin of the Prince of

Wales's plumes: the popular tradition which assigns it to the accidental fall of a lady's garter is pretty generally rejected, yet, as it does not appear that gentlemen wore garters at that period, it seems probable that the old tale may have been true. However this may be, the knights of the Garter were distinguished by a particular dress, consisting of a mantle, tunic, and capuchon, of the fashion of the time, all of blue woollen cloth; those of the knights companions differing only from the sovereign's by the tunics being lined with minever instead of ermine. All the three garments were powdered, that is to say, thickly embroidered, with garters of blue and gold, the mantle having one larger than all the rest on the left shoulder, enclosing a shield argent, with the cross of St. George, gules. Edward III. had 168 garters embroidered on his tunic and capuchon! Salades, differing from the bascinet in having a projection over the neck behind, were generally worn. The weapons of the knights of this period were chiefly lances, swords, maces, and battle-axes. Fire-arms were introduced in this reign, and cannon were used at the siege of Puy Guillaume in 1338, and in the English expedition against Scotland in 1337; but it is doubtful if any were used at Cressy, which battle was fought in 1346. The monumental effigy of Humphrey de Bohun, Earl of Hereford, is the first specimen of plate armour with taces, or overlapping plates (Sir S. Meyrick says), to envelope the abdomen. Soon after 1400, chain-mail was disused and the complete armour of plate adopted. The following interesting anecdote, though not relating exactly to dress, may not be much out of place.

Froissart relates the manner in which Edward III. presented a chaplet of pearls to the gallant French knight, Sir Eustace de Ribeaumont:—
" When supper was over and the tables removed, the king remained in the hall amongst the English and French knights bareheaded, except a chaplet of pearls which was round his head; when he came to Sir Eustace de Ribeaumont he assumed a cheerful look, and said, with a smile, 'Sir Eustace, you are the most valiant knight in Christendom that I ever saw attack his enemy or defend himself; I never yet found any one in battle who, body to body, had given me so much to do as you have this

day. I adjudge to you the prize of valour above all the knights of my court, as what is justly due to you.' The king then took off the chaplet, which was very rich and handsome, and placing it on the head of Sir Eustace, said, ' Sir Eustace, I present you with this chaplet as being the best combatant of this day, within or without doors; and I beg of you to wear it this year for the love of me. I know that you are lively and amorous, and love the company of ladies and damsels, therefore say wherever you go that I gave it you.'"

Another anecdote of this reign is on record, as follows:—While the English army lay encamped on the river Wear, Earl Douglas, with 200 men-at-arms, crossed the stream at some distance above their position. Advancing at a cautious and stealthy pace, they entered the English camp; at every challenge of the fixed sentinels Douglas exclaimed, " No ward? Ha! St. George!" as if to chide their negligence. Each soldier on the spot thought this to be a reproof of the nightly rounds directed to himself, and thus Douglas and his band passed on until he came to the royal tent, into which it is said he entered, and aimed a blow at the sleeping monarch of England, which was warded off by his chaplain, who was slain by interposing his own body. The king leaped up, seized his sword which hung at the head of his couch, the alarm was given, and Douglas made good his retreat through the English host with some loss. In this reign Rymer states, that the king having ordered 1000 men to be raised and trained with lances, 500 in North Wales and 500 in South Wales; he also directed the chamberlains of North and South Wales to purchase a sufficient quantity of cloth for making one suit for each man, consisting of a tunic and mantle, the cost of which should be allowed in their accounts at the Treasury; after this, it seems, that the captains used to stop part of the soldiers' pay to purchase necessaries, and for other purposes for them. This is probably the first time English troops have been clothed by the government.

RICHARD II.

A.D. 1377—1399.

THE march of foppery was accelerated under the reign of the weak and luxurious Richard of Bordeaux. "Fashions from proud Italy," and many imported by Queen Anne from Bohemia, infected even the menial servants. "The vanity of the common people in their dress was so great," says Knighton, "that it was impossible to distinguish the rich from the poor, the high from the low, the clergy from the laity by their appearance: all classes appear to have run into the extreme of absurdity in dress. In this reign the shoes were snouted and picked (piked) more than a finger long, crooking upwards, which they call *crackowes*, resembling devils' claws, and fastened to the knees with chains of gold." This is a quotation from an anonymous work of the time called the "Eulogium." The long-toed shoe was no novelty, but fastening the toes to the knee was new. No great variation took place either in the form of the armour or of its material, but generally it partook of the sumptuous extravagance of the age. The era of plate may be said to commence from the accession of Richard II. The camail, the gussets of chain at the joints, and the indented edge of the chain apron, are all that remain to be seen of the double-ringed mail worn at the commencement of the century. Milan was the great emporium from whence the most splendid suits were forwarded to the chivalry of Europe. The armour made expressly for Henry, Duke of Hereford, to wear in the famous duel at Coventry, was manufactured at Milan. The jupon and military girdle worn in the last reign were still worn; but the loose surcoat or blouse seems to have come again into fashion at the close of this century. It is generally, however, represented as fancifully embroidered instead of being emblazoned like the jupon: such is the surcoat on Richard II. in Plate No. X. The knight on the left of the Plate wears a bascinet of a novel and peaked shape, projecting from the face like the beak of a bird: it is rare, there are only two now known to exist.

X.

A.D. 1377 1399.

These knights are both taken from effigies: that on the right of the Plate is John de Montacute, in Salisbury Cathedral. The terms hauberk and haubergeon in this reign occasioned a good deal of confusion, from the circumstance of both the military garments originally so called being superseded by defences of plate, to which the old names were applied. Hauberk and haubergeon no longer designated chain or ringed armour only; the jambeaux or jambs (leg pieces) were sometimes made of *cuir-boulli*, a preparation of leather much used at this period, not only for armour, but for effigies and various works of art. The manner of a tourney in this reign is thus described by Froissart:—" Then issued forth of the Tower, about the third hour of the day, sixty coursers, apparelled for the justs, and upon every one an esquire of honour riding a soft pace. Then came forth sixty ladies of honour, mounted upon palfries, and every lady led a knight with a chain of gold. Those knights which were of the king's party had their armour and apparel garnished with white harts, and crowns of gold round the harts' necks; and so they came riding through the streets of London to Smithfield, with a great number of trumpets and other instruments of music before them. The king and queen, who were lodged in the Bishop's Palace of London, came from thence with many great persons, namely Valerian, Earl of St. Paul, that had married King Richard's sister; the Lady Maud Courtney; William, the young Earl of Ostravent, son to Albert of Bavaria, Earl of Holland and Hainault, with many others, and placed themselves in chambers to see the justs. The ladies that led the knights were taken down from their palfries, and went up into chambers prepared for them. Then alighted the squires of honour from their coursers, and the knights in good order mounted upon them; and then the helmets were set upon their heads, and being ready in all points, proclamation was made by the heralds, and the justs began. Many commendable courses were run, to the great pleasure of the beholders. These justs began on the Sunday next after the feast of St. Michael, and continued many days with great feasting and merriment."

The tabard seems to have become more general during this reign; it was an upper military garment, and continued in fashion till the time of Henry VIII. It was a species of tunic, which covered the front and back of the body, but was generally open at the sides from the shoulders downwards. From the time of its first introduction it was used by the military; afterwards it was emblazoned like the surcoat with armorial bearings.

The English archers were accustomed to draw the arrow to the eye or the ear, a method that has greatly the advantage over drawing it to the breast. The Irish archers, at the latter end of this reign, were habited in tunics, with a conical skull-cap, and had round quivers for their arrows at their right hips, which were confined by a broad belt round the body.

The French in this reign, intending to invade England, made a wall of wood, twenty feet high, and at every twelve feet was a tower large enough to hold ten men; these towers were ten feet higher than the rest, the whole extended 3000 paces, and were to have been brought over by ships to defend their men from the arrows of the English archers; but their ships being taken by the English, the wall was brought to Sandwich, and there put up, " to our great safety and the repulse of the Frenchmen."

HENRY IV.

A.D. 1399—1411.

In the fourth year of this reign it was found necessary to revive the sumptuary laws enacted, but to so little purpose, by his predecessors. They were revived, and with considerable additions, but with no effect. No person, not being a banneret or person of high estate, was permitted to wear cloth of gold, cloth of crimson, or cloth of velvet, or motley velvet, or large hanging sleeves, open or closed, or gowns so long as to touch the ground, or to use the furs of ermine, lettice, or martin, excepting only " gens d'armes quant ils sont armez;" an odd exception at first sight, but it alludes to the loose surcoat over the armour, and the caps and hoods that were worn till the trumpet sounded, and the bascinet was hastily assumed for action. Decorations of gold and silver were forbidden to all who possessed less than two hundred pounds in goods and chattels, or twenty pounds per annum, unless they were heirs to estates of fifty marks per annum, or to five hundred pounds' worth of goods and chattels. Four years afterwards it was ordained that no man, let his condition be what it might, should be permitted to wear a gown or garment cut or slashed into pieces in the form of letters, rose-leaves, and posies of various kinds, or any such like devices, under the penalty of forfeiting the same; and the offending tailor was to be imprisoned during the king's pleasure. These statutes were as little regarded as ever.

A decoration made its appearance in this reign, and was worn by the distinguished of both sexes, the origin of which is differently accounted for. The decoration is the collar of SS or esses. Camden says it was composed of a repetition of that letter, which was the initial of Sanctus, Simo, Simplicius, an eminent Roman lawyer, and that it was particularly worn by persons of that profession. Other writers contend that it was an additional compliment of Edward III. to the Countess of Salisbury. But its not appearing till this reign, is a sufficient answer to that supposition. There are various other suggestions on the subject.

It is a singular circumstance that the origin of such popular and celebrated decorations and badges as the feathers of the Prince of Wales, the order of the Garter, and the collar of SS, should to this day be a mystery to the most learned and indefatigable antiquaries.

There is no novelty to remark in the military dress of this reign, except that the soleret or steel shoe was sometimes supplied by footed stirrups, and the jambs or leg-pieces in such cases terminated at the instep. Increase of splendour is however visible. A rich wreath or band surrounds the bascinet of the knight, and the border of the jupon is cut into elegant foliage, in spite of the prohibition by statute.

Shere-peddin, a Persian cotemporary, and historian to Timour Bec, describing his battle with Bajazet, the Ottoman sultan, in 1401, states that in his army were 20,000 cavalry of Europe, all armed in steel from head to foot, so that nothing but their eyes were seen. Their armour was fastened below the foot by a padlock, which, except they open, their cuirasses and helmets could not be taken off.

In the year 1400, Manuel, Emperor of Constantinople, visited England, in hopes of securing succours from Henry IV. Of the English, he says, " The natives are bold and hardy, renowned in arms and victorious in war; the form of their shields or targets is taken from that of the Italians, and their swords from the Greeks. The use of the long bow is the peculiar and decisive advantage of the English." An instance occurs during the reign of Henry IV., showing the warlike character of the age. The Lady Spenser, a widow, accused the Duke of York of treason; and in proof of her assertion, produced her champion, William Maidstone, and offered to be burnt (the usual punishment) if he should be vanquished: the Duke accepted the challenge, but Henry imprisoned him, and thus prevented the fight. Froissart speaks of bascinets of this period being fastened behind thus : " He put his bascinet on his head, and then the squire laced it behind." He also speaks of a chapelle-de-fer, and a Montauban hat, fine, clear, and shining, all of steel. Chaucer, in his Canterbury Tales, thus describes a squire's yeoman : " He bore a mighty bow, and beneath his girdle appeared a bundle of sharp bright arrows, plumed with peacock's feathers; and upon his arm he wore a *gay bracer* (meaning an ornamented one) : to his baudrick, or sash of green, was appended a horn: besides this, he had on one side of him a sword and buckler, and on the other a gay dagger, harnessed well, and sharp as point of spear." The most memorable circumstance with regard to the bow which occurred during the reign of Henry IV., was the victory gained by the Scots, near Haledown-hill, in the year 1402, where, in the words of an old historian, " The Lord Percie's archers did withall deliver their deadly arrows so lively, so courageously, so grievously, that they raune through the men at armes, bored their helmets, pierced their very swords, beat their lances to the earth, and easily shot those who were more slightly armed, through and through :" and according to Atterborne, rendered it unnecessary for the men-at-arms to draw their swords. In the seventh year of this reign, arrow-smiths were compelled to boil and braze, and harden at the points with steel, the arrow, under pain of the forfeiture of all such heads otherwise manufactured, and imprisonment to the makers; and all arrow-heads to be marked with the maker's name. Arrows, as well as other missile weapons, were considered artillery. The baudrick seems to have been worn by the cross-bow men as well as the archers. In 1414, there was a weapon called harsegaye, which was a kind of demi-lance.

HENRY V.

A.D. 1411—1422.

THE civil costume of this reign scarcely differed from its immediate precursors. The military costume is remarkable for the introduction of the panache, the decoration of feathers having hitherto been confined to heraldic crests upon helmets, and never appearing as an ornament in England till this reign, though it appeared on the civil bonnet or hood in the time of Edward III. The bascinet underwent a change at this time, taking the shape of the head behind, and approaching the form of the salade. The large crested helmet was now only worn for the tournament. The jupon and military belt were still worn, but not so frequently: and the military effigies and illuminations of this reign are without jupon and surcoat. Taces were introduced, which are steel plates suspended from the breastplate. Another peculiarity of the period, was the custom of wearing large hanging sleeves of cloth, silk, or richer materials, with the armour; and it is not clear from the illuminations whether the body-armour conceals the rest of the garment, or whether they are merely sleeves fastened to the shoulder. When the sleeves were not worn, the shoulders appear to have been covered with overlapping plates, called *pauldrons*, and two circular plates, called *palletes*, are sometimes fastened to them in front, to protect the armpit. Lance-rests, in the form of hooks, are characteristic of this reign. St. Remy, a writer who was present at the battle of Agincourt, describes Henry himself, at break of day, hearing three masses, one after the other, armed in all his armour, excepting that for his head and his *cote d'armes* (i. e. emblazoned surcoat and jupon). After masses had been said, they brought him the armour for the head, which was a very handsome bascinet, a barierre (query baviere), upon which he had a very rich crown of gold, circled like an imperial crown—that is, arched over; the earliest instance of an arched crown worn by an English monarch. Monstrelet tells us the archers were for the most part without armour, and in jackets, with their hose loose, and hatchets and swords hanging to their girdles; some, indeed, were barefooted, and without hats or caps. Their jackets were pourpoints, and some of the caps made of boiled leather (the cuir-boulli) or wicker-work, crossed over with iron. Two-handed swords, with waved blades, first appear in this reign, but they were used more for state than war. A poleaxe was generally carried by commanders from this period to the reign of Edward IV. The bascinet had nothing to protect the face, by which it may be concluded that the umbril was put on and taken off at pleasure. On one side the elbow pieces are attached large fan-like ornaments, to protect the arm when straightened. The girdle is not used, but instead, a baudrick, or ornamental belt, coming from the right hip to the left thigh diagonally, and to this is appended the sword. Among the military instruments of war used at this period, was one called *coullart*: it was for the purpose of casting great heavy stones. Cannon were now used.

There was a kind of cannon called a bombard. Froissart mentions an extraordinary one used at the siege of Audinarde, made by the people of Ghent: it was fifty feet long, and threw stones of a wonderful bigness; when discharged it might be heard five leagues by day and ten by night, making so great a noise, "it seemed as if all the devils in hell were abroad."

"A Treatise on Pyrotechny," by Marcus Græcus, taught Friar Bacon in 1270, that the composition of gunpowder was two pounds of charcoal, one of sulphur, and six of saltpetre, well powdered in a mortar.

Henry V. in his seal is represented in complete plate armour, and his horse has the manifare, or protection for the horse's neck. The champfrein takes a different form from that of the last reign, and not only wraps round the nose, but has likewise cheek-plates; it reaches only just above the nostrils.

From Rymer's "Fœdera" we learn the terms and manner in which an English army was raised, in 1415, for the expedition to France. Contracts were made by the keeper of the privy seal with different lords and gentlemen, who bound themselves to serve, with a certain number of men, for a year, from the day on which they were first mustered. The pay of a duke was 13s. 4d. per day; an earl, 6s. 8d.; a baron or banneret, 4s.; a knight, 2s.; an esquire, 1s.; an archer, 6d.; and each contractor received 100 marks for every thirty men-at-arms. A duke was to have fifty horses; an earl, twenty-four; a baron or banneret, sixteen; a knight, six; an esquire, four; an archer, one: the horses to be furnished by the contractor, the equipment by the king. All prisoners were to belong to the captors; but if they were kings, the sons of kings, or officers of high rank bearing commissions from kings, they were to belong to the crown on the payment of a reasonable recompense to the captors—this practice was introduced by Edward III. The booty taken was to be divided into three parts, of which the leader took two and left the third to the king. The visors of bascinets were at this time frequently termed ventails.

The privilege of distributing prizes and remitting the punishment of offenders was, by the laws of the tournament, invested in the fair sex; but at the justs their authority was more extensive. The justs were usually made in honour of ladies, who presided as judges paramount over the sports; hence arose, in the spirit of romance, the necessity for every true knight to have a favourite fair one, who was not only esteemed as the paragon of beauty and virtue, but supplied the place of a titular saint, to whom he made his vows, and addressed himself in the day of peril. This feeling was not confined to military pastimes, it animated warriors in the day of battle. "Oh that my lady saw me now!" said one of them, as he was mounting a breach at the head of his troops and driving the enemy before him. The victory of Agincourt in the year 1415 is in great measure ascribed to the English archers; and that there might be no want of arrows, Henry V. ordered the sheriffs of several counties to procure feathers from the wings of geese, picking six from each goose. An archer of this time was clad in a cuirass, or a hauberk of chain-mail, with a salade on his head, which was a kind of bascinet, but projecting much behind, and upon which was a movable visor; he had a sabre suspended at his side. Fabian describes the archers at the battle of Agincourt thus: "They had their limbs at liberty, for their hose were fastened with one point, and their jackes were long and easy to shoot in; and that they might draw their bows of great strength, and shoot arrows of a yard long besides the head, every man had a good bow, a sheaf of arrows, and a sword;" and it is said that each archer bore on his shoulders a long stake sharpened at both ends, which he was instructed to fix obliquely in the ground before him, thus to oppose a rampart of pikes to the charge of the French cavalry. The cross-bows at this time were made strong enough to send the quarrels forty rods. In Plate XI. the archer and cross-bow man is pourtrayed; the former clad in a hauberk of mail, the latter, who is winding up the string by a moulinet and pulleys, is dressed in a leathern jacket with mamellieres, or plates of iron on his breast, as well as on his elbows. There were other arbalisters who wore helmets, and are represented with a large heart-shaped shield, called a pavise, hanging on their backs, and a case of quarrels at their right hip, or attended by a pavisier, whose duty it was to ward off the missiles of the enemy. The cross-bow was a complicated and expensive weapon, and consequently often carried by the sons of knights, who were attended by one of their father's retainers, who carried the pavise. During the reign of King James I., a cross-bow man was regarded as on a level with a knight, a distinction in those days of great importance. "We enact that no knight's son, who is not a knight himself or a cross-bow man, shall sit at table with knights or their ladies."

XI

A.D. 1399—1422

In besieged castles cross-bow men were placed behind the crenelles, which were the turrets pierced with holes for them to shoot through. They were frequently called creniquineers, and their cross-bows crenequins. At the battle of Agincourt, having chosen a convenient spot on which to marshal his men, the king sent privately 200 archers into a low meadow, which was on one of his flanks, where they were so well secured by a deep ditch and marsh, that the enemy could not get near them; then he divided his infantry into three squadrons or battles, the avantguard composed entirely of archers, the middle ward of billmen only, and the rear ward of archers and billmen mixed; the horsemen, as wings, went on the flanks of each battle. Stakes about five or six feet long were placed in the ground, and hid by the archers standing before them. When the heavy cavalry of the enemy charged, which they did with great impetuosity, under the idea of riding over and cutting down the archers, they shrunk behind the stakes, and the French, unable to stop their horses, were overthrown and put to the utmost confusion. The infantry who were to follow up hesitated, being lost in amazement. During the panic the English archers threw back their bows, and with axes, bills, glaives, and swords slew the French till they met the middle ward, and the victory became complete. The light cavalry of this time were still called hobilers, as the heavy were men-at-arms. There were men-at-arms, hobilers, archers, both horse and foot, and infantry. Speed mentions, that there were with the English 1600 Irish kernes enrolled from the Prior of Kilmainham, able men, but almost naked: their arms were darts and swords, their horses small and had no saddles, yet they were nimble, and played with the French in spoiling the country, rifling houses, and carrying away children, with their baggage on cows' backs.

M. de Bonucant says, that the King of England used cannon at the battle of Agincourt, which threw panic into the French army, being strangers to them; this, however, was not the case, for the French had used them before the English; and it is positively asserted by Livius Ferozilienus d'Elmham that the French were drawn up thirty deep, and had within their lines cannon. Hand-guns were first used in the year 1414 at the siege of Arras.

HENRY VI.

1422—1461.

THE dress of the people generally of this reign was a mixture of all the fashions of past ages, with every thing the most ridiculous and extravagant that could be invented or discovered at the moment. The dress of the knights of the Garter was altered in this reign; the colour of the surcoat and chaperon was changed to scarlet, and afterwards back to white; the number of garters to be embroidered on them was limited to 120 for a duke, and less in proportion to rank, down to a knight bachelor, who wore sixty. The king was unlimited, and on Henry's surcoat and hood there were 173. The armour partook of the fantastic and ridiculous caprices of the day; surcoats and jupons were less worn: the jazarine jacket was frequently worn in lieu of the breast and back-plates; this defence was composed of small overlapping plates of iron covered with velvet, the gilt studs that secured them forming the exterior ornament. To the bascinet helmet and chapel-de-fer was now added a new head-piece called a *salade* or *sallet* : its principal characteristic is the projection behind. The armour in general is exceedingly ornamented; the spurs, sometimes of enormous length, were screwed to the heel instead of being fastened with leathers. The shield of this reign was made with a projection above and below, to prevent the lance, when struck against it, slipping down and injuring the thigh. Hand-guns had, as already mentioned, been used at the siege of Arras, in the year 1414, and in this reign they were coming into more general use; but they were very rude in construction, being formed of a simple iron tube with a touch-hole at top, fixed in a stock of wood about a cubit and a half long, and called the frame of the *goune*. It was soon found that the priming fell off by the touch-hole being at the top; a hole was therefore made at the side and a small pan put under to hold the priming, and a cover for the pan was invented on a pivot to turn off and on; it was thus used in England as early as 1446, as appears from a roll of purchases for the castle on Holyland. An act of parliament was passed in this reign wherein captains were forbidden to stop any part of the soldier's pay, except for clothing; that is to say, if he was waged for half a year, 10s. for a gown for a gentleman, and 6s. and 8s. for a yeoman, upon pain of 20l. for every spear and 10l. for a bow to the king. The spear was the weapon carried by a gentleman, the bow by a yeoman, and soldiers were denominated from the weapons they carried. At the battle of St. Albans, the army of the Queen of Henry VI. and the Earl of Warwick, as well as that of the Duke of York, were distinguished by badges; a mistake concerning them gave the victory to the latter. Besides badges the soldiers frequently wore distinguishing scarfs.

The cross-bow was used at this period, made of hard wood, ornamented with ivory; they were about three feet three inches long, the steel bow about two feet eight inches from end to end, weighing fifteen pounds; the length of the groove for the quarrel about one foot four inches. The arrows discharged were called both quarrels and viretons— some with feathers, others without. The vireton is a French name; the feathers being set on a little curved, made it spin round as it passed through the air.

In the Record-office of the Tower of London is an indenture of retainer, whereby Sir James Ormond, knight, retains Mr. James Skidamore, to serve under him in the expedition against France, under Richard, Duke of York, in the nineteenth year of this reign, by which he is bound to serve for a year in all places where it shall please Sir James to order him as a man-of-arms, with six archers in his company, all on horseback and well-chosen men, well and sufficiently armed, horsed and arrayed, every man after his degree: Sir James to have harness complete, with bascinet or salade, with visor, spear, axe, sword, and dagger; and all the archers good jakks of defence, salades, swords, and sheaves of forty-one arrows at least. Sir James to have 19d. per diem, with the accustomed reward; and for each of the archers 6d. per diem. A quarter's wages to be paid in advance, and a second quarter of a year's wages when he shall make the first muster of himself and men on the sea-side, or where Sir James shall order him; and for the other half year, to be paid in France, the muster to be made on the day and place to be named by the Duke of York: and the said James Skidamore to take for himself and archers cloaks of the said lord the duke's livery, paying for them like as other soldiers of their degree do. Sir James Ormond to have the third part of the winnings of war of Mr. James Skidamore, and the third of the archers during the said time; and James Skidamore to have all prisoners taken by him or his archers, except kings, kings' sons, princes, and other captains, and men of kings' blood, or having their power, the which shall be prisoners to Sir James Ormond, he paying a reasonable sum for them.

During this reign, May 29th, 1430, the Maid of Orleans was burnt: it is said she wore man's armour.

The English were not backward in the encouragement of archery; in 1453, the Parliament voted an army of 20,000 bow-men for service in France. The battle of St. Albans seems to have been won entirely by the archers; the men-at-arms never once engaged.

There was a cloak used in France during this reign, called a *paletocques*, from which is probably derived the paletot now used in England. The jacque, or jakk, which some of the archers used, appears to have been made with pieces of leather overlapping each other.

There were many jousts and battles fought in this reign before the king. John Upton and John Downe fought in Smithfield: the battle did not last long, for the king, persuaded of the innocence of the one party and the loyalty of the other, put a stop to it. At Paris, Sir John Astley maintained a duel on horseback against Peter de Masse, a Frenchman, in the presence of Charles VII. of France: he pierced the said Peter through the head, and took his helmet to present to his lady. Another fight took place in Smithfield, before the king, between Sir John Astley and Sir Philip Boyle, an Arragonese knight; this was fought on foot, with battle-axes, spears, swords, and daggers. Sir John Astley vanquished the knight, and his jacque is now in the armoury of Sir Jacob Astley at Melton-Constable. In 1442, and again in 1446, another fight took place. Defeat in these battles was considered a proof of

XII

A D 1422.—1461.

guilt, and the death of one party was strong evidence that the other's cause was true. The vanquished, if accused of treason and killed, was adjudged to the punishment of a convicted traitor, and his body, whether alive or dead, underwent the act of hanging, in order that his posterity might participate in his infamy. A curious case, where the vanquished party was slain, and still underwent degradation, is that of a *jouste à outrance*, in 1387, between Jacques le Gris and Jehan de Caronge: a lady was accused of treason and adultery, and her cause espoused by her husband; had he been conquered, his wife would have been burnt, and he would have been hanged; but it chanced that he was victorious. Lances and javelins were used at this period, as well as pole-axes, long swords, and large rowelled spurs—mottoes were sometimes written on the shanks. The espiet, espiot, or espien, called by the Spaniards espeton, was likewise used; also the glaive, which was a kind of sword-blade fixed to the end of a short staff. The mounted figure in Plate XII., which is drawn from one in the Tower, has a glaive in his hand; it is supposed to have been the armour of Henry VI. The figure on foot in this Plate is taken from the monumental effigy of Robert, Lord Hungerford, which is in Salisbury Cathedral: he died in 1455—a splendid specimen of the armour of that period. Some of the light cavalry at this time wore loose boots, and had merely slips of steel put over their hose and pantaloons, terminating in ornamental knee-caps; their arms protected in a similar manner, and their shoulder-plates were so ornamented as to represent the wings of a bird; the guard of the sword was turned up before and down behind. The shields were fancifully made in the shape of a heart: targets and circular shields were also used. The toes were pointed down, as they had been from the time of the Conquest, and continued so to Henry VII.'s reign, when they were elevated. The men-at-arms often used to dismount and fight on foot.

In 1432, several kinds of artillery are mentioned, cannons, bombardes, vulgaires, coulverins. The vulgaires were ordinary artillery. In the year 1460, James II. of Scotland was killed by the accidental bursting of a cannon. The artillery of the Turks, in the year 1453, surpassed whatever had yet appeared in the world. A stupendous piece of ordnance was made by them; its bore was twelve palms, and the stone bullet weighed about 600 lbs.; it was brought with great difficulty before Constantinople, and was flanked by two almost of equal magnitude: fourteen batteries were brought to bear against the place, mounting 130 guns: the great cannon could not be loaded and fired more than seven times in one day. Mines were adopted by the Turks, and counter-mines by the Christians. At this siege, which was in 1453, ancient and modern artillery were both used. Cannons, intermingled with machines for casting stones and darts, and the battering-ram was directed against the walls. The fate of Constantinople could no longer be averted: the diminutive garrison was exhausted by a double attack; the fortifications were dismantled on all sides by the Ottoman cannon; a spirit of discord impaired the Christian strength. After a siege of fifty-three days, Constantinople, which had defied the power of Chosroes, the Chagan, and the Caliphs, was subdued by the arms of Mahomet II. This is part of Gibbon's spirited account of the siege.

EDWARD IV.

A.D. 1461—1483.

EDWARD IV. was a great warrior. Philip de Comines gives him the following character: "King Edward was a man of no great forecast, but very valiant, and the beautifullest prince that lived in his time." The new fashion that Edward chose for his last state dresses, was to have them made with very full hanging sleeves, like a monk's, lined with the most sumptuous furs, and so rolled over his shoulders as to give his tall person an air of peculiar grandeur. He altered the surcoat and chaperon of the order of the Garter from the white cloth of the last reign to purple velvet. There was at this period no fashion so ridi-

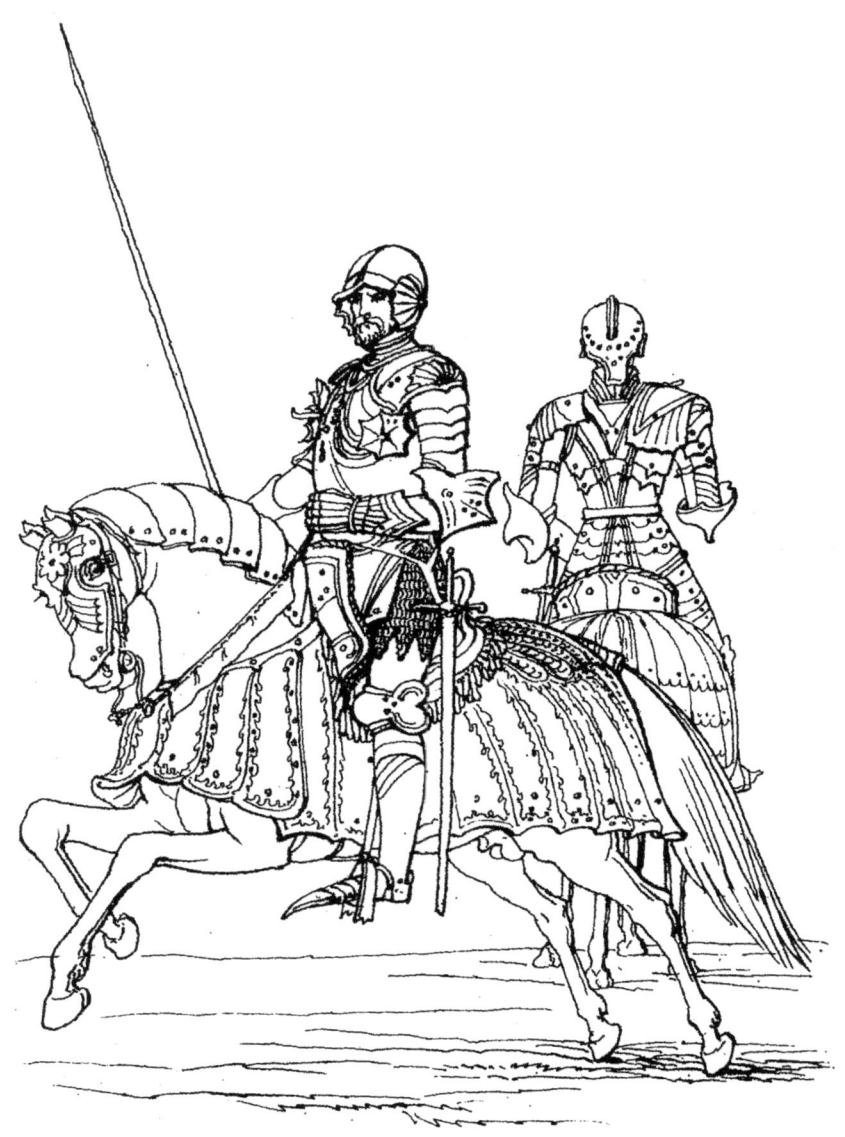

A D 1461,—1485.

culous started in France, but then, as now, it was immediately adopted in England. The jackets, doublets, or pourpoints, were cut shorter than ever, and the sleeves of them slit, so as to show their large, loose, and white shirts; the shoulders were padded out with large waddings, called *mahoitres;* and so capricious were the beaux of the period, that he who to-day was shortly clothed, was habited to-morrow down to the ground. They wore the hair so long that it came into the eyes; and they covered their heads with bonnets of cloth a quarter of an ell or more in height. Toes of the shoes were worn a quarter of an ell long, called *poleines*. Paradine says, " the men wore shoes with a point before half a foot long; the richer, and more eminent persons, wore them a foot, and princes two feet long, which was the most ridiculous thing that ever was seen: and then, when tired of these, they adopted others, called duck-bills, having a bill four or five fingers in length. Afterwards they wore slippers, exceeding in front of the toes a good foot."

No one under the rank of a lord was allowed to wear the indecently short jackets, gowns, &c., mentioned by Monstrelet, or pekes or poleines to his shoes and boots exceeding two inches in length. In the military habit very globular breastplates, and large tuilles (only one for each thigh), terminating in a sharp angle, are characteristic of this reign: the sollerets, still enormously long and pointed, called poleines: the visored salade is the general head-piece of knights in battle. The morion first appears in this reign. The skull-caps of steel, called *casquetels* and *capelines*, with the large oval ear-pieces, are frequent; and the gorget and apron of chain-mail are escalloped at the edges. See Plate XIII., in which two knights of this reign are pourtrayed, taken from the Tower of London. The jazerine jacket, and nearly all the armour of the preceding reign, may be found in illuminations of the present. Halberts are first mentioned about this period. The *voulge*, a variety of glaive or guisarme, and the *genetaire*, a kind of Spanish lance, are added to the offensive weapons; and the hand-gun became common. Swords and bucklers are first assigned to archers in this reign. Chamfreins, for the horses' heads, with spikes projecting from them, were adopted about

1467. In the celebrated battle fought at Towton against superior numbers, King Edward ordered his archers to shoot a volley of arrows, which were used for great distances, and then retire a little; the consequence was, when another was returned from the Lancastrians, in whose faces the snow descended with great violence, they fell short of the mark. Fauconbridge, who commanded Edward's archers that composed the van, then ordered them to throw back their bows, and draw their swords; whereupon the armies met, and the battle became a furious conflict of personal strength and bravery, which was ultimately decided in favour of Edward.

In an illumination in the British Museum, there are represented soldiers with long tubes, which rest on their shoulders, and which they hold up by both hands, which seem to be hand-cannons. These tubes are bound round at different distances, being probably composed of two or more pieces, and thus held together. As this manuscript is embellished with a white rose, we may conclude it to be of the time of Edward IV. The helmets of the soldiers have large circular or oval earpieces, which distinguish the early part of this reign (see Plate XIII.). Besides these, there are dismounted men-at-arms, archers, and cross-bow men, the former in complete armour; but instead of a helmet they wear a *capeline*, the crown of which is convex, and the rim cut into angles; their gorgets and aprons of chain-mail are vandyked, and their breasts protected by two demi-placards over the plate, and of different colours. The archers have black or purple pantaloons, shirts of mail with short sleeves, and over their close vests vandyked, and the tight sleeves of the under garment cover the rest of the arms: some carry their arrows in a girdle at the right hip, and some have them in quivers. The cross-bow men are habited somewhat in the same way, except that instead of salettes with large oreilletes, they have salades with movable visors, and wear their cases containing the bolts or viretons on their right hips. Their large arbalestes wind up somewhat in the same manner as that drawn in Plate XI., but instead of the handles being one up and the other down, they are both the same way. The lances of the cavalry at this period were of excessive length, and when held out for charging, scarce any part projected beyond the elbow, as heretofore had been the case, and which so greatly tended to counterbalance the weight. In this reign an act was passed ordering every Englishman to have a bow of his own height, and butts were ordered to be put up in every township for the inhabitants to shoot at on feast days, and if any neglected, the penalty was one halfpenny. By the 24th of Edward IV., bows of yew were to be sold for 3s. The brigandine jacket took its name from a light-armed irregular troop called brigands; it was composed of square iron plates quilted with linen, and continued to be used by archers from the latter part of Henry the Sixth's reign to that of Elizabeth inclusive (see Plate XIX.). At the latter end of this reign the tabard was made quite loose. The helmet of Henry Green, who died in the year 1467, has the visor in the middle of the ventaille, with perforations above and below for the sight and breath.

Feathers are mentioned as worn by the men-at-arms in the year 1473. Pierre de Rohan, seigneur de Gié, is represented with a tremendous feather like a fox's brush, hanging from a pipe on the top of his helmet, low as almost to touch his horse behind. In 1463 troops were armed with capelines. The sword blades in the time of Edward IV. were nearly flat, but in earlier times a section of them would have presented the figure of a lozenge: they tapered from the guard gradually to the point to the reign of Henry VIII. In Henry the Seventh's time they had a ridge on each side, and at the commencement of Henry VIII., instead of a ridge were thickened towards the point.

There was a grand fight in 1467 before the king, between the bastard of Bonjouie and Lord Scales, brother to the queen, both on horse and foot. Lord Scales had the best of it; and other jousts and tiltings took place with pointless lances, which were used in opposition to the real and sanguinary jousts, called "joustes à outrance," or, as Froissart calls them, "joustes mortelles et à champ." The following is an amusing extract; how a man shall be armed at his own ease when he shall fight on foot:—

"He shall have none shirte on him, but a doublet of fustian, lyned with satin, but full of holes; the doublet must be streightly bound, the poynts must be sett about the great of the arme, and the vest before and behynd; and the gussets of mail must be sewed into the doublet, into the bought of the arme and under the arme; the armyng points must be made of fyne twyne, such as men make strings for cross-bows, and they must be trussed small and poynted as poynts; also they must be waxed with cordwainer's wax, and then they will not breke: also a peir of *stamyn*, single, and a peir of short bulworks of thyn blanket, to put about the knees for *chanfying* of his leg harneis; also a peir of shone of thyck cordewayne; and they must be *frette* with small whipcorde, three knots on a corde, and three cordes must be fast sewed into the shoo, and fyne cordes in the myddil of the sole of the same shoo; and that there be between the *frettes* of the heel, and the *frettes* of the myddil of the shoo the space of three fingers." Then comes the method of arming a man. The knight began to put on his armour from his feet upwards. 1st, his sabotyna, or steel clogs; 2nd, the greaves, or shin-pieces; 3rd, the cuisse, or thigh-pieces; 4th, the breech of mail; 5th, the millettes, or overlapping pieces below the waist; 6th, the breastplate, or cuirass; 7th, the vanbraces, or cover for the arms; 8th, the rerebraces, or arrière bras, the covering for the remaining part of the arm to the shoulders; 9th, the gauntlets; 10th, the dagger was hung; 11th, the short sword; 12th, the cloak or coat which was worn over the armour; 13th, the bascinet; 14th, the long sword; 15th, the pennoncel, held in the left hand; 16th, the shield. The foregoing is taken from the "Archæologia," vol. xxii; it is written in old language. When the pennoncel is held in the left hand, it is added, " paynted of St. George or of our Lady, to blesse him with as he goeth towards the felde, and in the felde." A plate of Montfaucon's, intended to represent the battle of Rosebreque, represents many of the combatants as wearing jazerine jackets instead of cuirasses; but the rest of the armour made of plate. Many of the figures have the plate-armour ending at the ancles, and solerets only of jazerine work. Doublets were at this time worn, and often over armour, as may be seen in Montfaucon's Works. The price charged by a London tailor at this period for making one of these doublets, with lining, for the use of the king, was 6s. 8d.

The first introduction of hand-guns into England seems to be when King Edward landed at Ravenspur, in Yorkshire, in the year 1471: he brought with him 300 Flemings, armed with "hande-gonnes."

When gunpowder was first discovered to have a projectile power, its military application was confined to a kind of mortar, or bombard, intended as a substitute for the enormous battering machines then in use. Vilari asserts that they were used at the battle of Cressy; the more accurate Froissart is entirely silent about them.

EDWARD V.

There was little time for change in this short reign.

RICHARD III.

A.D. 1483—1485.

Richard the Third's wardrobe was at all times magnificently furnished, he and the Duke of Buckingham being notorious for their love of dress and finery. A mandate still exists amongst the Harleian MSS., sent from York by Richard to the keeper of his wardrobe in London, dated August 31, 1483, wherein he specifies the costly habits in which he was desirous of exhibiting himself to his northern subjects, with a descriptive detail, which, as Mr. Sharon Turner justly remarks, "we should rather look for from the fop that annoyed Hotspur, than from the stern and warlike Richard III." The king wore the crown on his head at the battle of Bosworth, and chancing to espy Henry, Earl of Richmond, spurred his horse forward, exclaiming, "Treason! treason! treason!" He slew with his own hand Sir William Brandon, the bearer of the hostile standard, struck to the ground Sir John Cheney, and made a desperate blow at his rival, when he was overpowered by numbers, thrown from his horse and slain, Lord Stanley taking up the crown, placed it on the head of Richmond, and he was instantly greeted with shouts, " Long live King Henry!" No higher degree of perfection in armour was ever attained than during this reign; the pauldrons almost assumed the appearance of the later pass-guards; the knee and elbow-pieces were much longer, generally fan-shaped, and of most elaborate workmanship. The *salade* and the hausse-col, or gorget of steel, was still worn, the former sometimes surmounted by the knight's chapeau and crest. The tilting shield is still more fantastic in shape, and the war shield has become almost pentangular. The sword is belted, so as to hang almost in front, and the dagger is attached as usual to the right hip. The armour pourtrayed in Plate XIV. was worn probably with little variation during this reign, though the Plate is placed in the reign of Henry VII., being more of that date than this; the fluted suit of armour is in the Meyrick collection, and is rare; the mounted figure is a beautiful specimen in the Tower of London. The third figure is Sir John Cheney, who, as already mentioned, was struck down by Richard III. in Bosworth Field. The drawing is made from his monumental effigy in Salisbury Cathedral: he died in 1509.

Leather jacks, jazerine jackets, and short linen or cloth doublets, the latter generally white with St. George's cross upon them, with long hose, are the general habits of the archers, billmen, and guisarmiers; their head-piece being a salade, or a round iron pot helmet, or skull-cap. A statute passed in the first year of this reign, complaining that, owing to the seditious confederacy of the Lombards using divers ports of this realm, the bow-staves were raised to an outrageous price, to eight pounds a hundred, when they were wont to be sold at 40s. This act, therefore, provides, that ten bow-staves shall be imported with every butt of Malmsey or Tyre wines brought from Venice, under a penalty of thirteen shillings and fourpence for every butt of the said wines in case of neglect.

XIIII.

A D 1485.—1509.

HENRY VII.

A.D. 1485—1509.

"At the close of the fifteenth century," says Strutt, "the dress of the English was exceedingly fantastical and absurd, insomuch that it was even difficult to distinguish one sex from the other." There were terms applied to male apparel which our ears are accustomed to as indicative of women's dress.

The author of the "Boke of Kervynge," quoted by Strutt, says, "Warme your soveraine his petticote, his doublet, and his stomacher, and then put on his hozen, and then his schone or slippers, then stryten up his hozen mannerly, and tye them up, then lace his doublet hole by hole," &c. The fashion of slashing makes its appearance about this time. The shoes were now worn absurdly broad at the toes, as they were previously pointed. The hair was worn enormously long and flowing, the faces shaved, old men and soldiers only wearing moustaches.

The fluted armour in Plate XIV., as already observed, is a rare specimen, but it partakes of the character, in every respect, of the armour of this period. The breastplate is globular and of one piece, so is that of Sir John Cheney in the same Plate. The sollerets are widened at the toes in accordance with the new fashion of the shoes, armour invariably taking its general form from the civil costume of the day. The helmet assumes the form of the head, having movable lames or plates at the back to guard the head, and yet allow the head to be thrown back with ease: this is shown in the mounted figure in Plate XIV. The helmet opened to receive the head by throwing up the *mentonnière*, or lower part which guarded the chin, as well as the visor which turned on the same pivot. The panache was changed in this reign for the plume, inserted in a pipe fixed at the back of the helmet, just above the neckplates, and consisted of a profusion of feathers, sometimes streaming down the shoulders almost to the crupper of the horse, as represented in the seal of Henry VIII.

The pass-guard was introduced in this reign, being plates rising perpendicularly upon the shoulders to ward off a thrust at the side of the neck. The halberd is now a weapon in common use, and halberdiers appear for the first time amongst the English infantry; an improvement in fire-arms took place, by fixing on the hand-gun a cock to hold the match, and from that circumstance called the arc-a-bouche or arc-a-bousa, corrupted into arquebus. Henry VII., on establishing the body of yeomen of the guard in 1485, armed half of them with bows and arrows, and the other half with arquebuses.

The men-at-arms sometimes carried a semicircular concave shield with a very large boss; their elbow-pieces terminated in sharp points, and had to their salades, when worn without the hausse-col, cheek-pieces formed of several successive plates with hinges. The armour of this date in the Tower is worthy of notice. The large puckered plates of steel which cover the thigh to the knee, and continue behind, except where hollowed out for the saddle, are the greatest curiosity. A billman in this reign wore a jazerine jacket and a salade. Cloaks were frequently worn with armour from the time of Edward II. to that of Charles I. Sir John Cheney wears a cloak in his effigy, as shown in Plate XIV.

In the year 1485 Henry VII. raised the yeomen of the guard, which may be considered as the first formation of a regular standing military force in England. Rapin, who calls them archers, says they were instituted on the day of his coronation, and that they consisted of fifty men to attend him and his successors for ever. By the first regulation, every yeoman of this band was to be of the best quality under gentry, well made, and full six feet high. Their numbers have varied under almost every reign, and originally consisted of a certain number in ordinary, and an indefinite number extraordinary, and in case of a vacancy in the former, it was supplied out of the latter number; half, as before stated, carried bows, and half arquebuses, and they all had long swords. A part of them were armed with halberts in the time of Henry VIII., when they acquired their present form of clothing (see one in Plate XVIII.). The archers in the illuminations of this period are clothed in a shirt of mail, with short wide sleeves, such as that worn by the cross-bow men in the time of Henry VI., and probably not differing much from the figures in Plate XI. of the time of Henry V.; but they wore over the shirt of mail a small vest of red cloth, laced in front, with pantaloons or tight hose on their legs, and braces on their left arms. The conduct of the English archers under the Lords Dawbeney and Morley, at the battle of Dixmude, in 1489, is worthy of remark. They attacked the French camp, though defended by a strong battery, poured a volley of arrows into the trenches, fell on the ground till the guns had been discharged, rose on their feet, poured in a second volley, and rushed precipitately into the camp. Such was the resolution of these troops, that John Person, of Coventry, having lost his leg by a cannon-shot, continued to discharge his arrows, kneeling or sitting; and when the Frenchmen fled, he cried to one of his fellows, and said, "Have those six arrows that I have left, and follow thou the chase, for I may not."

The cross-bow of this reign consisted of two kinds: the latch, with its wide and thick bender for quarrels, and the prodd for bullets. Towards the close of his reign, Henry VII. forbade the use of the cross-bow: his object was to induce more frequent practice in archery. In his youth he had been partial to this exercise; he continued to amuse himself with the bow after he had obtained the crown, as is seen by the following memoranda in an account of expenditure: "Lost to my Lord Morging at the butts, 6s. 8d., and paid to Sir Edward Boroughe, 13s. 4d., which the kynge lost at buttes with his cross-bow." Both his sons followed his example.

There is an instance mentioned of horses having armour for the legs, being short pieces of overlapping plates on the upper part of the legs. The spontoon, a wide-bladed spear, came into use in this reign. The battle-axe at this time was considered a royal weapon, and was borne as such at the funeral of Henry VII. and Queen Mary, and solemnly offered up at the altar with the helmet, gauntlets, and crest.

The favourite colours of the House of Tudor were green and white, therefore with these Henry VII. tinged the ground of one of the standards he set up at Bosworth Field, whereon was painted a red dragon, in allusion to his descent from the Welsh king Cadwaladyr. On his arrival in London after his victory, Henry offered up his banner in the church of St. Paul, as a trophy, and in further commemoration of his success, instituted the office Rouge Dragon poursuivant-at-arms. The uniform of the English soldiers during this reign was white, with a red cross upon it. In the disastrous battle of St. Aubin, Sir Edward Wydeville was slain with all his countrymen, and 17,000 Bretons who, to deceive the enemy, had adopted the white coats and red crosses of the English troops.

The following indenture gives a full idea of the various kinds of troops forming the English armies in 1492. It begins, "This indenture, made between the King our sovereign lord, Henry VII., by the grace of God, King of England and France, and Lorde of Irelande, on that oon partie, and his right trusty and right well beloved cousin George, Earl of Kent, on that other partie, witnesseth," &c. &c. It goes on to say that he, the Earl of Kent, is to serve in the wars beyond sea, &c. &c., with a retinue and number of six men-at-arms, his own person included, and each of them having with them his custrell and his page, sixteen demi-lances, twenty-one archers on horseback, sixty archers on foot, of good and able persons for the war, horsed, armed, garnished, and arraied sufficiently, &c. &c.; of which retinue, the said earl is to make his musters at Guildford the 4th day of June next; and on arrival at Portsmouth, he is to receive the conduyte money due for bringing the said retinue there; that is to say, 6*d.* for every twenty miles from their home to Portsmouth. The pay of each man-at-arms, with his custrell and page, 1*s.* 6*d.* per day, and for each demi-lance 9*d.* per day. The earl to receive a month's wages for the whole on arrival at Portsmouth, the month reckoned at twenty-eight days, and he is to pay his retinue when embarked; and at the end of the month he is to receive another month's pay for the month ensuing, and so forth from month to month during the *reteyndre* with our said sovereign. And the earl and his retinue were bound to serve according to a certain book of statutes and ordinances of war " made by our said sovereign lorde, by the advice of such lordes of his blode, capitaynes of his armie, and other folk as be of his counsell." There are numerous similar indentures with other persons of rank, to bring a certain number of troops, and serve the king beyond sea for a whole year. In this way about 1700 men were then raised, though probably a much larger force in other ways. It appears that the army was divided; the cavalry into men-at-arms, with their custrells and pages also mounted, demi-lances and horse-archers; the infantry consisted of bowmen, billmen, and halberdiers. This last kind of troops first made their appearance in this reign; the distinguishing mark of their weapon from that of subsequent periods was that the axe blade had a diagonal termination. When Henry VII. created his son Henry Prince of Wales, four gentlemen offered their services upon the occasion. First, they made declaration that they did not undertake this enterprise in any manner of presumption, but only "for the laude and honor of the feaste, the pleasure of the ladyes, and their own learning and exercise of deedes of arms, and to ensure the ancient and laudable customs."

At the battle of Fournone in 1495, there were German arquebusiers on horseback and on foot. The arquebus underwent an improvement at this time; hitherto, like the arbalaste, it had a straight stock to hold the barrel, but now it was formed with a wide butt end, which might be placed against the right breast. It was afterwards called a hackbutt or hagbut; the smaller sort were called demi-hags. At the battle of Fournone the number killed on both sides by fire-arms did not exceed ten.

Description of PLATE No. XV., *containing Helmets.*

No. 1, the helmet of Robert, Duke of Normandy, eldest son of William I., of the year 1096.

No. 2, helmet of the time of Edward I., 1280.

No. 3, helmet of John of Eltham, second son of Edward II., who died in 1334.

No. 4, from the monumental effigy of Sir William Stainton, the reign of Edward II., 1326.

No. 5, reign of Edward III., 1370.

No. 6, time of Henry IV., 1399.

No. 7, time of Henry V., 1413.

No. 8, a salade of time of Henry VI., 1450.

No. 9, a very curious open-work helmet of Henry VI.'s time, 1450.

No. 10, casque of Richard III.'s time, 1483.

Nos. 11 and 12 are jousting helmets.

No. 13, a cap which was worn under the jousting helmet.

No. 14, a helmet found in Bosworth Field, of Richard III.'s reign.

No. 15, time of Henry VIII.

Nos. 6, 7, 8, 9, 10, 11, 12, 13, and 15, are in the Tower of London.

XV

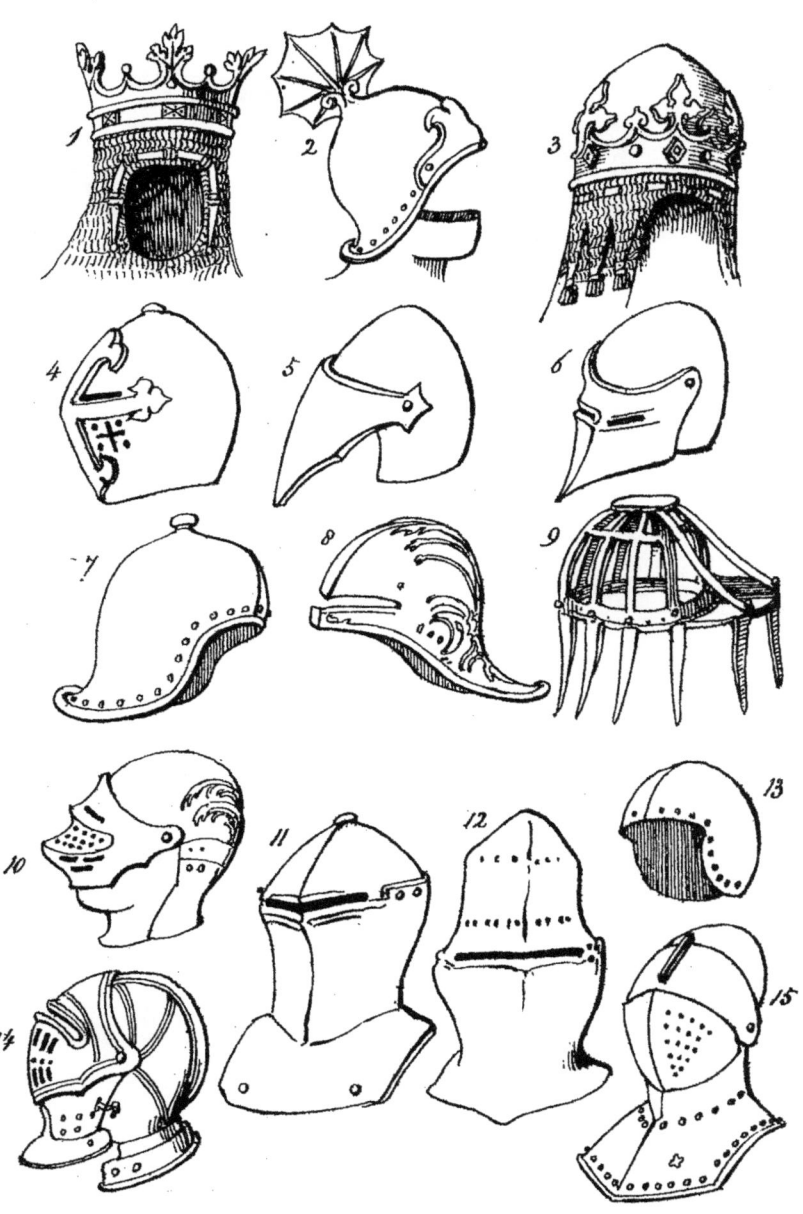

A.D. 1096—1520.

HENRY VIII.

A.D. 1509—1547.

HENRY VIII. was splendid in dress. Soon after his accession, the close hose, fitting exactly to the limbs, in fact the Norman chausses, were again revived under the still older name of *trouses;* and he is described by Hall as wearing, at a grand banquet given at Westminster in the first year of his reign, a suit of " shorte garments, little beneath the pointes, of blew velvet and crymosyne, with long sleeves, all cut and lyned with cloth of gold, and the utter parts of the garments powdered with castles and sheafes of arrowes (the badges of his Queen Catherine) of fyne dokett (ducat) golde; the upper part of the hosen of like sewte and facion; the nether parts of scarlet, powdered with tymbrelles of fine golde. On his head was a bonnet of damaske silver, flatte woven in the stoll, and thereupon wrought with golde and ryche feathers in it." In the twenty-fourth year of his reign, Henry VIII. passed a sumptuary law, confining the use of furs of black genets to the royal family, and furs of sables to the nobility above the rank of a viscount, &c. &c.

Howe, the continuator of " Stow's Chronicle," states that Henry VIII. never wore any hose but such as were made of cloth. In an inventory of his apparel, however, preserved in the Harleian library, we find mention of several pair of silk hose :—" one short pair of black silk and gold woven together," &c. &c., and an amazing variety of rich and very expensive dresses are enumerated.

Camden, in his " Remains," tells a pleasant story of a shoemaker of Norwich, named John Drakes, who, during this reign, coming to a tailor, and finding some fine French tawny cloth lying there, which had been sent to be made into a gown for Sir Philip Calthorp, took a fancy to the colour, and ordered the tailor to buy as much of the same stuff for him, and make him a gown of it, precisely of the same fashion as the knight's, whatever that might be. Sir Philip arriving some time afterwards to be measured, saw the additional cloth, and inquired who it belonged to. "To John Drakes," replied the tailor, "who will have it made in the selfsame fashion as yours is made of." "Well," said the knight, "in good time be it; I will have mine as full of cuts as the shears can make it," and both garments were finished accordingly. The shoemaker, on receiving his gown slashed almost to shreds, began to swear at the tailor, but received for answer, "I have done nothing but what you bade me; for, as Sir Philip Calthorp's gown is, even so have I made yours." "By my latchet," growled the shoemaker, "I will never wear a gentleman's fashion again."

Hair had been worn exceedingly long during the last reign. Henry VIII. gave peremptory orders for all his attendants and courtiers to poll their heads; and short hair, in consequence, became fashionable. The collar and the great and lesser George, as at present worn, were given to the knights of the Garter by Henry VIII., who reformed the statutes of the order, and altered the dress. The surcoat was made of crimson velvet, and a flat black velvet hat of the fashion of the time superseded the chaperon, which was, however, still worn for ornament only, hung over the shoulder, and thence called the *humerale*; it was of crimson velvet, the same as the surcoat. The lesser George was not worn before the thirteenth of this reign, when it hung in a chain of black riband on the breast.

The armour of this period was rich in decoration. The lamboys were continued throughout this and the following reign; but when they are not appended to the breastplate, tassets and cuisses, composed of several plates instead of one, are seen on the thigh. There is in the Tower a magnificent suit of armour, which was presented by Maximilian I. to Henry VIII. on his marriage with Catherine of Arragon; the complete suit both for horse and man is beautifully engraved with legendary subjects, badges, mottoes, &c., and is the same in shape as a suit in the Belvedere Palace at Vienna. Raised armour, the forerunner of the embossed, was introduced in this reign. Puffed and ribbed armour is also occasionally met with (see Plate XVIII.). The breastplate was still globose, but towards the middle of the reign, rose to an edge down

XVI.

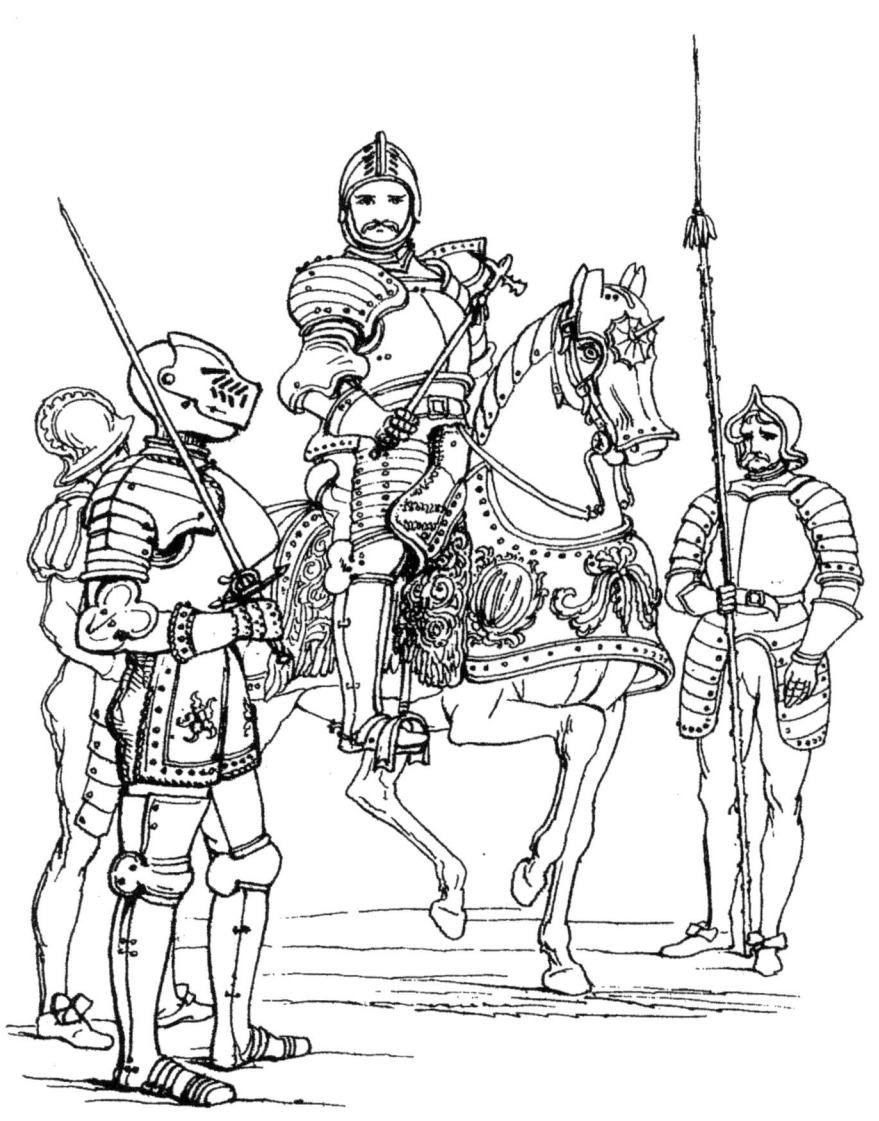

A D 1509 — 1547.

the centre, called the tapul, a revival of an old fashion. Towards the end of the reign the breastplate presented a salient angle in the centre. The tilting helmet disappeared altogether about this time, and a head-piece, called a coursing hat, was worn with a mentonnière. The helmet was adorned with streaming plumes. The gauntlets were mostly made with overlapping plates without fingers.

The *hackbut*, first mentioned in the reign of Richard III., now became common, and the *partizan*, a variety of pike, was used. The wheel lock was added to the matchlock. The pistol and its variety, the dag or tacke, are also of this period. Pikemen composed the principal part of the English army from this reign to that of William III. Fluted armour continued to be worn till the middle of this reign; and although there is but one specimen in the Tower of London, yet all the men-at-arms are thus equipped in that curious old painting given by his late Majesty to the Society of Antiquaries, representing the battle of Spurs, which was fought on the 10th of August, 1513.

Plate XVI. represents Henry VIII. mounted, in a suit of armour, which is in the Tower, and which is said really to have belonged to the king. The armour is damasquined, and consists of tilting helmet, gorget, back and breastplates with placcate, garde-de-reins, pauldrons with pass-guards, rere and vanbraces, gauntlets, tassets, demi-cuisses with genouillères, jambs, and sollerets. In his right hand is a martel-de-fer. The horse armour is not of the same pattern as the body armour. The stirrups are curious from their great size. The men on foot are of the same period, but the figure in the foreground has a most extraordinary breastplate projecting almost to a point; his tassets are also very curious and uncommon. The helmet is likewise singular.

The battle of Spurs, of which a drawing is already mentioned, should be called the battle of Guinegate, the name of the place where it was fought, but the French made so much use of their spurs, that it has been so called ever since. Lords Shrewsbury and Herbert were before Terouenne, an inconsiderable place, which they were besieging. Henry VIII. arrived in camp from Calais, and the Emperor Maximilian joined him with 4000 horse. Louis XII., determined to relieve the town, was advised not to hazard his person in battle. The French cavalry, which had been collected at Blangy, dividing into two bodies, advanced along the opposite banks of the Lis, under the Dukes de Longueville and Alençon. Henry had the prudence to consult the experience of his imperial ally, who was acquainted with the country, and had already obtained two victories on the same ground. By his advice the army was immediately mustered, Maximilian hastened to meet the enemy with the German cavalry and the English mounted archers, while the king followed with the principal part of the infantry. The French gendarmes, formed in the Italian campaigns, who had acquired the reputation of superior courage and discipline, fled on the first shock of the advanced guard; the panic went through the whole army, and 1000 of the best cavalry in Europe were pursued about four miles by the German and a few hundred English horse. Their officers, in the attempt to rally the fugitives, were abandoned. Embrecourt and another, though taken, were fortunate enough to make their escape; but the Duke de Longueville, the Marquis de Rohelin, the Chevalier Bayard, Busy d'Amboise, Clermont, and La Fayette, warriors distinguished in the military annals of France, were secured, and presented to the united sovereigns.

Henry was skilful with the two-handed sword; when he was twenty years of age he repeatedly fought at the barriers with the two-handed sword, or the battle-axe, and was always successful. He served as a volunteer with the Emperor Maximilian, and adopted troops called lansquinets, which were used by the emperor in 1543. He had 2000 of these soldiers.

The martel-de-fer were of various shapes, frequently handsomely ornamented; when not used they were carried at the saddle-bow. At the interview between Henry and Francis I., at the Champ de drap-or, where a grand tournament took place, the English archers and captain of Henry's guard kept the ground on the French king's side, and the captain of the French king's guard, his archers, and Swiss troops, kept the English king's side, and suffered none to enter but the combatants. The French troops were clothed in blue and yellow, with the badge, a salamander, embroidered thereon.

In the Cotton library is a manuscript of Henry VIII.'s time, very curious, but too long to copy in a work like this. It describes "the order to be had when the king goes to battle; the forwarde of the battle to be in order as followeth; the ordynance of the kyng when he goeth to battayle; the order of the kyng if he intend to fyghte; how to maintayne a duke in battayle, and in what arraye; how to maintayne an earle in battayle; how to maintayne a baron; how to maintayne a bannerett:" and then follows "how to ordeyne battayles, and to arrange the hoste."

1st.—They must not be set too thick together, lest one should encumber the other.

2nd.—Not too thin, lest the light-armed of the enemy should easily enter amongst them to annoy them.

3rd.—To set the best armed, strongest, and best weaponed men in front, the weakest in rear.

4th.—The general may divide his army into four or five battles, as he may see occasion; but if the enemy be stronger than himself, he should bring all his men together, and endeavour to force in upon the enemy unawares.

Seven precepts showing when the enemy may be strong:—

1st.—When they are assembled in good order.

2nd.—When they have the advantage of any passages of water, mountains, strayths, &c.

3rd.—When the wind, the sun, or the dust is in their backs.

4th.—When they assail their opponents suddenly, while at meat or otherwise employed, thinking themselves secure.

5th.—If they have been some time at ease, untired with long marches, watches, &c.

6th.—While they hold together in firm league, without dissension and quarrels.

7th.—If they are well acquainted with the state and condition of their adversaries.

By statute 3 Henry VIII., all men under the age of forty, some certain persons only excepted, were ordered to have bows and arrows, and to use shooting; and in the thirty-third year of his reign, another act passed ordering all men under sixty, except spiritual men, justices, &c., shall use shooting with the long bow, and shall have a bow and arrows ready continually in their house. That every person having a man child or men children in his house, shall provide a bow and two shafts for every such man child being seven years old and upwards, till of the age of thirteen, in order to promote shooting. No person under seventeen shall use a yew bow, under penalty of six shillings and eightpence, unless he have lands of the value of 10*l*. yearly. Aliens are prohibited from shooting without the king's licence, and shall not transport bows into foreign countries. In the twentieth year of his reign, Henry instituted a society for the practice of shooting, under a charter, in the name of the fraternity of St. George; and he granted to this fraternity the privilege, that if any of the members shooting at a known and accustomed butt, having pronounced the word "fast," or " stand fast," should happen to kill any body passing between the shooter and the butt, he should not suffer or be imprisoned. It was in this reign that archers had two strings to their bows. The archers at this time wore a small buckler on their sword hilts, which had been the custom since the time of Henry VI.

In the memoirs of the Marquis de Flemange, it is stated that the English archers used mallets in 1524; and in the ancient poem of the battle of Flodden Field, leaden mallets are several times mentioned; they appear to have been tremendous weapons in the hands of strong, active men.

The partizan, a kind of pike, before mentioned, was found more useful than the pike in mounting breaches, and in attacking and defending lodgments. It continued during Elizabeth's time. Shakespear says, "Let us make him with our pikes and partizans a grave." It was used as late as William III., and is carried by our yeomen of the guard. In the procession of Henry to meet Francis I. at Ardres, he is represented as preceded by billmen, who are followed by the yeomen of the guard with *pertusians*, and next his henchmen, and the rear brought up by demi-lances. The march of this monarch against his enemies is thus described in a book in the Cotton library: "first go a strong party of horse, guarded on both sides by two cannons, attended by two troops of horse, one to the right, the other to the left; then follow a large party of harquebusiers, and henchmen ranked alternately, preceded by a small, and followed by a large, party of harquebusiers only; and at both ends as wings is a small guard of archers, and on the right and left several pieces of cannon. Then the main body composed of pikemen and henchmen, flanked with archers, and on each side a large wing of horsemen well armed. The king's person is guarded by henchmen. After the main body follows a detachment of harquebusiers, then a larger one, flanked by archers, and followed by another party of harquebusiers, and on each side many pieces of cannon. The rear is brought up by the baggage, women, and cattle, guarded by a strong party of cavalry."

The standard of the earl marshal at Flodden Field, 1513, was red, and had on it three goats' heads couped, with the motto "Veritas vincit."

Stubbs describes the doublets of the sixteenth century as reaching down to the middle of the thighs, though not always quite so low, "being so hard quilted, stuffed, bombasted, and sewed, as they can neither work nor yet well play in them. Through the excessive heat and stiffness thereof, therefore are forced to wear them loose about them. They make their bellies appear to be thicker than all their bodies besides; they are stuffed with four, five, or six pounds of bombast at the least, and made of satin, taffita, silk, grograine, gold, silver, and what not, slashed, jagged, cut, pinched, and laced with all kinds of costly lace of sundry colours."

There were two kinds of ordnance at this period. Field pieces, the smallest were twelve-pounders; a cannon of battery, from a culverin to a whole cannon; and these were again subdivided into falconet, falcon, minion ordinary, minion largest, saker least, saker ordinary, demi-culverin, &c. Hitherto, the ordnance used by the English was made by foreigners; but in the year 1521, says Stow, "John Owen began to make brass ordnance, as cannons, culverins, and such like: he was the first Englishman that ever made that kind of artillery in England."

The first bomb-shells appear to have been made in 1543, when "Henry, minding wars with France, made great preparations, as well of munitions and artillery; and one Peter von Cotton, a gunsmith, conferring with Peter Bawd, desired to be made certain mortar pieces, being at the mouth eleven inches unto nineteen wide, for which he made certain hollow shot of cast iron, to be stuffed with fireworks, whereof the bigger sort has screws of iron to receive a match and carry fire to break in small pieces the same hollow shot, whereof the smallest piece hitting a man would kill or spoil him."

Henry VIII. instituted the first permanent corps of cavalry, and denominated it "the band of Gentlemen Pensioners." His object was to form an honourable body-guard, on which he could perfectly rely; and, at the same time, to create a nursery for officers of his army, governors for his castles and fortified places; his orders and regulations on this occasion are preserved in the Cottonian library, written on fine quarto leaves of indented vellum. Every one of the said gentlemen was to be complete in harness and habiliments, to have two double horses, for himself and page, also his coutrell (an attendant armed with a long knife), with a javelin, a demi-lance, well armed and horsed. That every of the aforesaid men-at-arms shall furnish and make ready two good archers, well horsed and harnessed; the wages of the spears and archers to be paid at the end of every month; every spear, for himself, his coutrell, page, and his two archers, 3s. 4d. sterling per day. The lieutenant for wages and for entertaining himself, his coutrell, page, and six archers, 6s. per day. The men-at-arms and their company to be mustered by the captain or lieutenant every quarter of a year, or at such time as the captain or lieutenant may order. They took an oath of allegiance to the king; these regulations are without date, but supposed to have been made in 1509, the first year of his reign. The original number of men is not mentioned, but most of the chronicles fix it at fifty. The establishment, however, being found too expensive, the corps was disbanded a short time after its institution, and before the year 1526, revived on smaller pay; and they appear to have done duty on foot in the court with poleaxes, the same, probably, as at present used. They had two standards, one of St. George's cross, the other, four hands; the blazonry is not mentioned.

The globose breastplate, with but slight edge in the centre, was succeeded by one where the edge was more raised, and made to project in the centre of the breast; the projecting part was afterwards moved lower down. The flexible cuisses were composed of pieces overlapping each other upwards, that if a lance should strike the thigh, it may glance off, instead of passing between the plates. The cuisses of officers of infantry extended only half way down the thigh, and the sole armour for the arms were epaulettes, which reach nearly to the elbow, but only protect the outside. The figure on foot on the right in Plate XVI. has a gorget of plate, an open casque with ear pieces, and gauntlets.

In 1512, having issued his commission to the Earl of Shrewsbury to raise an army to oppose an invasion, the king desires him to give the soldiers such badges as he may think most desirable. An army raised in the thirty-sixth year of his reign, was ordered to be thus clothed:—
" First, every man sowder to have a cote of blew clothe, after such fashion as all fotemans cotes be made here in London, to serve his majestye in his journey; and that the same be garded with redde clothe, after such sort as others be made here, and the best sene (*i. e.* best looking men) to be trimmed after such sort as shall please the captain to desire; provided always, that noe gentleman nor other wear any manner of silk upon the garde of his cote, save only upon his left sleeve, and that no yeoman wear any manner of silk upon his said cote, nor noe gentleman nor yeoman to wear any manner of badge. Every man to provide a pair of hose for every of his men, the right hose to be all red, and the left to be blew, with one stripe of three fingers, broad red, upon the outside of his leg from the strike downwards. That every man have an arming doublet of fustian or chanvass, and every man to have a cap to be made to put his sculle or salette in, after such fashion as I have desired, which William Taylor, capper, doth make for me, where

you may have as many of them as you list for 8*d*. a piece." The badge then appears to have been set aside, and a red cross was ordered to be sewn on the uppermost garment, upon pain of fifteen days' imprisonment; and this was further inforced on a man's going in "hostinge or battayle;" it was called the cross of St. George. The coat of the soldier, however, appears to have been white.

The statute of Henry VII., in 1508, was now renewed for prohibiting the cross-bow; but the cross-bow was afterwards included under the head of artillery. There were long-bows, cross-bows, slur-bows, and stone-bows, scorpions and catapults. The use of gunpowder and improvement in gunnery superseded the cross-bow as a weapon of war; though Father Daniel says there was but one arbalester at the fight of Bico, but so skilful was he, that an officer, named Jean de Cardonne, having opened the visor of his helmet to take breath, this man struck him in the unguarded part with his arrow, and killed him! So at the siege of Turin, in 1536, though there was but one arbalester in the grand army, yet he was so expert that he killed more persons than any of those using the arquebus. In a curious and rare journal of the Protector's expedition to Scotland, written by W. Patten, who was joined in commission with Cecil, as Judge-Marshal of the army, and printed in 1548, he writes relative to the Scots at that time. "Their armour and their manner, as well going to offend as of standing to defend, I have thought necessary here to utter. Hackbutters have they few or none, and appoint their fight most commonly always on foot; they come to the field well furnished, all with jack and skull, dagger and buckler, and swords all broad and thin, of exceeding good temper, and universally so made to stree, that as I never saw none so good, so I think it hard to devise the better. Hereto every man his pike, and a great kercher wrapped twice round his neck, not for cold, but to prevent cutting; in their array towards joining with the enemy, they cling and thrust so near in the fore-rank, shoulder and shoulder together, with their pikes in both hands, straight afore them, and their followers in that order so hard at their backs, laying their pikes over their foregoer's shoulders, that if they do assail undiscovered no force can well withstand them. Standing at defence, they thrust their shoulders likewise so nigh together, the fore-ranks well nigh kneeling, stoop low before, their fellows behind holding their pikes with both hands, and therewith in their left their bucklers; the one end of their pike against the right foot, and the other against the enemy breast-high, their followers crossing their pike points with them forward; and thus each with other so nigh as space and place will suffer, through the whole ward so thick, that as easily shall a bare finger pierce through the skin of an angry hedgehog, as any encounter the front of pikes!" The length of the Scottish pike was, by act of the Parliament of 1476, to be six ells—about eighteen feet long. The mace was changed for the pistol in this reign.

There was a species of artillery at this period called war-carts, each carrying two pierriers, or chambered pieces; several are represented in the picture of the siege of Boulogne. They were used by the Scotch in 1471, when the barons and prelates were ordered to provide such carts against their old enemies the English. The small arms at this time were hand-guns, arquebuses, demi-haques, and pistols. It was enacted that no hand-gun should be used of less dimensions than one yard in length, gun and stock included. M. De la None says the Reiters first brought pistols into general use, which are very dangerous when properly managed; but the grand invention of this period was the wheel-lock, which continued in use to the time of Charles II.

The Honourable Artillery Company of London, now a corps of volunteers, was instituted in the year 1537, by Henry VIII., for the encouragement of archery. The earliest patent, however, on the incorporation of its present form is dated the 3rd of King James I., in 1606.

EDWARD VI.

A.D. 1547—1553.

THE principal distinction in the armour of this reign is the breastplate, which resembled a pea-shell, and was called the peascod belly. Bulwer calls the doublets "long peascod-bellied doublets," and observes, "when we wore short-waisted doublets, and but little lower than our breasts, we would maintain by militant reason that the waist was in its right place, as nature intended it; but lately we come to wear them so long-waisted, yea almost so long as to cover the belly," &c. The morion came into use; brigandine jackets were worn by archers, with steel skull-caps. Some armour in the Tower, of this period, does not show a great increase in the length of the waist. Plate XVII. represents a very handsome suit of russet armour on the figure mounted; the footman also wears a handsome and peculiar armour, with a morion on his head.

Edward VI. was fond of archery, which nevertheless began to decline during this reign. Hollinshed laments it in this curious manner: "In times past the chief force of England consisted in their long bows, but now we have in a manner given over that kind of artillery. Certes the Frenchmen and Reiters, deriding our new archery in respect to their corslets, will not let in open skirmish, if any leisure serve to turn up their tails, and cry 'shoote Englishmen,' and all because our strong shooting is decayed and laid in bed. But if some of our Englishmen now lived, who served King Edward III., the breech of such a varlet should have been nailed to his bum with an arrow, another feathered in his bowels," &c. &c.

Bishop Latimer, in his sixth sermon, condemns the vices of the age, and deplores the decay of archery, which he calls a "gyft of God, that he hath given us to excell all nations;" and again he says, "a wondrous thynge that so excellent a gyft of God should be so little esteemed;" and concludes by adding, "it is a goodly arte, a holesome kynde of exer-

XVII.

A.D. 1548—1553.

cise, and much commended in physike. Marcelus Sicenus, in his boke De Triplice Vita, (it is a great while since I read him now,) but I remember he commendeth thys kinde of excercise, and sayeth that it wrestleth against many kyndes of deseases. In the reverance of God let it be continued: let a proclamacion go forth, charging the justices of peace that they see such actes and statutes kept as were made for thys purpose."

The force of arrows is well instanced by a fact recorded in the journal of Edward VI. A hundred archers belonging to the king's guard shot at an inch board, singly two arrows each, and afterwards all together; some of these arrows pierced through this and into another board placed behind it, although the wood was exceedingly solid and firm. The distance at which they shot is not mentioned. An ancient bow, according to Neade and Père Daniel, would carry 400 yards. It is not surprising that archery, which had arrived at great perfection as to accuracy and quickness in shooting, should reluctantly be given up for fire-arms, which for a long time were exceedingly heavy and clumsy, slow in loading, troublesome in cleaning, and not fired with great accuracy.

There seems to have been a great variety of swords at this period. The braquemart or short sword, the French rencontre sword, the soccado or long sword, the espadon or two-handed sword, the Swiss or basket-hilted sword, a Spanish sword called the toledo, or, more properly, rapier, a tuck inclosed in a walking-stick, a poniard, a dagger, sabre, and scimeter. After the invention of fire-arms, instead of a boss or spike in the centre of shields, some were armed with small gun-barrels, an aperture being made above, and covered with a grating, for the convenience of taking aim. There is one in the Tower.

In an old account of the battle of Musselburgh, in Scotland, fought in the first year of this reign, the targets used by the Scotch are described; and the account continues, " and with these targets found we great rattels, swelling bigger than the belly of a pottle pot, covered with old parchment of dooble papers, small stones put into them to make a noys, and set upon the end of a shaft of more than two ells long, and this was their fine device to fray our horses, when our horses should cum at them. Howbeit, because the riders were no babies, nor the horses no colts, they could neither duddle the tone, nor fray the toother, so that the pollecye was as witless as the power forceless."

MARY I.

A.D. 1553—1558.

EARLY in this reign there was no alteration in armour from the preceding one; at the close, the only change was, that the breastplates were not quite so long.

The statute, 4th and 5th of Philip and Mary, repealing all other acts respecting keeping armour and horses, shows the quantity and kind of armour and weapons that were to be kept at that time by persons of different estates. All temporal persons, with an estate of 1000*l.* or upwards, shall keep six horses fit for mounting demi-lances, three of them to have sufficient harness, steel saddles (saddles whose bows and cantels were covered with steel), and weapons requisite and appertaining to the said demi-lances; and ten light horses, with the weapons necessary for light horsemen. Also forty coats of plate corslets or brigandines furnished, forty pikes, thirty long bows, thirty sheaf-arrows, thirty steel caps or skulls, twenty black bills or halberts, twenty harquebuts, and twenty morions or sallets.

In this way armour, arms, and horses were provided by persons according to the value of their estates temporal. A person having an estate worth 1000 marks is to maintain four horses for demi-lances, two of which to be with sufficient weapons, saddle mete and requisite to the said demi-lances, &c.; and the scale of property descends to 400*l.*, 200*l.*, 100*l.*, 40*l.*, 20*l.*, 10*l.*, and 5*l.* per annum, the latter being obliged to find one coat of plate furnished, one black bill or halbert, one long bow and one sheaf of arrows, and one steel cap or skull. Temporal persons having goods and chattels to a certain amount, from 1000 marks down to 10*l*., were also to find horses, arms, and armour in proportion to the value of such goods and chattels. Temporal persons, not charged by this act, having annuities, copyholds, or estates of inheritance, to the clear value of 30*l*., or upwards, to be chargeable with furniture of war according to the proportion for goods and chattels. The ladies were not exempt, for the following act was introduced: "Every person temporal, whose wife (not being devorced nor willingly absenting herself from her husband) doeth wear any gown of silke, French hood, or bonet of velvet with any habilement edged with golde, pearle, or stone, or any chain of gold about her necke, or in her partlet, or on any apparel of her body, except the sonnes and heires apparent of dukes, marquises, earls, viscounts, and barons, and others having hereditaments to the yearly value of 600 marks or above, during the life of their fathers; and wardes, having hereditaments of the yearly value of 200*l*., and who are not by this act before charged, to have, maintain, and keepe any horse, shall, from the first of May, have, keep, and maintain one able horse, meete for a light horseman, with sufficient harness and weapons for the same." Then the penalty is mentioned for not conforming with the act. Cities and boroughs, towns and parishes, were also to provide arms and armour. The justices of every county were authorized to make search for, and view from time to time the armour, arms, and horses to be provided. A heavy penalty was attached to a soldier making sale of his horse, harnesse, or weapons. From this we also learn that the military force of the kingdom, in the year 1558, consisted of demi-lances, with steel fronts and backs to their saddles, who supplied the place of men-at-arms, and instead of light, became heavy cavalry; of light horse, who replaced demi-lances; and of infantry of the following kinds of troops. The pikemen, who wore corslets, which consisted of a breastplate with tassets, a backplate, a gorget, a pair of gauntlets, and a steel hat. The archers, who wore each a pair of brigandines, (consisting of a back and breast formed of small plates of iron, sewn within some kind of quilted stuff, and generally covered with sky-blue cloth,) a steel skull-cap, a bow, and a sheaf containing twenty-four arrows. Black bill-men or halberdiers, who were clad each in a pair of almaine rivets, (made of small bands of plate laid over each other, with movable rivets on each side,) or else they wore coats of plate, which seem to have differed from the almaine rivets, merely by being made of bits of metal, and morions or sallets on their heads. And lastly, those who carried arquebuses.

In Plate XVIII. is represented a demi-lancer, and a man in puffed and ribbed armour, taken from a drawing of armour in the Meyrick collection, of an earlier date than this reign; and a yeoman of the guard, originally raised by Henry VII., afterwards altered and reformed in Henry VIII.'s reign, and put in the dress which the men retain at present called "Beefeaters." The rulers of this reign were not apparently anxious to introduce into general use fire-arms, but considered a long-bow equal to a harquebus. Although demi-lances appear to have done the duty that men-at-arms formerly did, yet the men-at-arms were not discontinued, though their dress is not mentioned; it is probable that their armour partook much of fancy, and was richly ornamented, or the reverse, in proportion to the wealth of the wearer. Their appellation seems to have changed to spears or spearmen.

The square toe of Henry VIII.'s time was continued to this reign. A proclamation was made by Mary, that no man should wear his shoes above six inches square at the toes! Peaked shoes came again into vogue, as shown by the Earl of Leicester's armour in the Tower of London.

Lord Wentworth, in a letter to Queen Mary, makes mention more than once of a kind of fire-arms called a currier, while writing respecting the siege of Calais. It was a kind of hackbut. Little notice is taken of it by military writers.

XVIII.

A.D. 1553–1558.

ELIZABETH.

A.D. 1558—1603.

EVERY one knows how fond of dress, and how magnificent was "good Queen Bess;" her great ruff, her jewelled stomacher, her portentous petticoats, were of more importance, and more thought of, than bringing a sister queen to the block. There are many records of the variety and splendour of Queen Elizabeth's wardrobe; but as this work is not intended to review the dress of ladies, we proceed to that of the gentlemen, in which there was a great change.

It was the age of big breeches; the large trunk hose, the long-waisted doublet, the short cloak or mantle with standing collar, the ruff, the hat-band, and feather, shoes with large roses, are all seen in the early paintings of this reign.

Strutt quotes the following curious note from a MS. in the Harleian Library: "Memorandum: that over the seats in the Parliament House there were certain holes cut, some two inches square, in the walls, in which were placed posts to uphold a scaffold round about the house within, for them to sit upon who used the wearing of great breeches stuffed with hair like woolsacks; which fashion being left off the eighth year of Elizabeth, the scaffolds were taken down, and never since put up." This may have been the case in the Parliament House, but certainly large breeches, *very* large breeches, were worn after Elizabeth's reign. James I. is always represented in a most preposterously large pair.

Stubbs assures us that no people in the world "are so curious in new fangles" as the English. He describes shirts worn that cost 10*l*. apiece; of ruffs, he says, "every body will have one, whether they can afford it or not, and sooner than go without will mortgage their land on Shooter's Hill, Stangate Hole, or Salisbury Plain; or risk the loss of their lives at Tyburn with a rope, in token whereof," he adds, "they have now (1595) newly found out a more monstrous kind of ruff, of twelve, yea, sixteen lengths apiece set three or four times double; and it is of some fitly called three steps and a half to the gallows." He then describes the trunk hose or breeches, and other parts of the dress; but we must leave the civilians, and see how this custom operated on military costume. It is distressing to observe how all the absurdities of fashion in civil life have been followed by the military, to the great discomfort and disadvantage of the soldier.

The armour of this reign seldom comes lower than the hips, complete suits only being used for jousting, and even then some knights appeared without armour for the legs. The breastplates were made thicker to be bullet-proof; the tassets of them began to be made of one plate each, though marked in imitation of several. The point of the tapul reappeared at the bottom of the breastplate, and projected downwards. Highly ornamented morions were worn.

Carabines, petronels, and *dragons* are frequently mentioned amongst the fire-arms of this reign. The *petronel* was so named from *poitrinal,* being fired with its straight and square butt-end held against the chest. The *dragon* was so called from having a dragon's head on its muzzle; and the troops who used it were called dragoons. The origin of the *carabine* or *carbine* is disputed. Troops called *carabins,* a sort of light cavalry from Spain, are first mentioned in 1559.

The coat of the soldier in the reign of Henry VIII. was white, with the red cross of St. George on the front. In 1584 Queen Elizabeth changed the colour, she having ordered 100 men to be raised in Lancashire for the Irish service, orders that the soldiers shall be armed with swords and daggers, and convenient doublets and hose, and also a cassock of some motley or other sad green colour or russet; also every soldier to have 5s. to provide a mantle in Ireland, besides his livery coat. This was the regulation for the infantry; but the cavalry wore a red cloak. The queen directed the Bishop of Chester and his clergy, who were to provide a part of 1000 lances, to be sent to the Low Countries, that " for their apparell (says the order), it shall be convenient that you see them furnished of redd clokes, lined, without sleeves, and of length to the knee, dobletts, hose, hatts, boots, and all other necessary apparell for their bodies."

There were great jousts in the month of April, 1560, mentioned by Stow. He describes the trumpeters thus: "there rode the trumpeters, blowing their trumpets, with scarfs of white and black sarcenet; also the two kings of arms, and the heralds Somerset, Lancaster, Richmond, York, Rouge Dragon, and more of them, had scarfs of white and black sarcenet about their necks."

The monumental effigy of Sir H. Bradburne, at this period, represents him with his cuisses opened, on account of the wide puffed breeches. The cuisses were made to separate, if necessary, at two different lengths, according to the size of the trunk hose, but united when worn in battle, and with a chain mail apron under them.

A constant apprehension of an invasion from Spain during the first part of Elizabeth's reign, induced the queen to be very attentive to her internal forces. She issued instructions for the execution of the commission directed to all the justices of peace, by which they were to attain perfect knowledge of the numbers, qualities, abilities, and sufficiency of all her subjects, from the age of sixteen years upwards, that may be found able to bear armour, or to use weapons on horseback, or on foot; and out of the total number, being viewed, mustered, and registered, to select the most able, and to be by the inhabitants of every shire tried, armed, and weaponed, taught and trained, to use and handle their horses, armour, shot, and other weapons, both on horseback and on foot, for the service and defence of her majesty, her crown, and realm, against all attempts both inward and outward, &c. Men were not omitted who could serve as labourers or pioneers, also as carpenters, smiths, or such like artificers, so that there may be some use had of their abilities, for the service of the country, as cause shall require, though they shall not have armour. Prelates, lords of parliament, and privy-councillors were exempt from serving, but they were bound to send able servants, and household men with their armour and weapons, and horses. Poor people who had not sufficient value of goods or freehold property to furnish one whole furniture of armour and weapons, were "to be treated withall by good persuasion and for the love of their countrie," to be induced to join together by two or three, or more, in the provision of a furniture, either of a pikeman, archer, or arquebusier, to serve as occasion shall require; and, "furdermore, they shall persuade all manner of riche farmours and freeholders to keep in their house persons mete for archerie and shott." In the distribution of weapons, in every 100 footmen, there were to be at least forty arquebusiers and twenty archers. There existed a law against shooting with hand-guns and arquebuses; but those appointed by the commissioners to be arquebusiers, were to use their weapons without danger of the laws.

In Plate XIX. there is a demi-lancer in armour to his knees, a pikeman, and arquebusier, with breastplates, tasses and morions on their heads. Two archers are in the foreground, wearing brigandine jackets and morions on their heads. A very particular account of the clothing of the army employed in Ireland in 1559 is given by Sir John Harrington: he says, "I must not forget nor cease to tell her majesties good, wise, and gracious providings for us her captains and our soldiers, in summer heats and winter's colds, in hunger and thirst, for our backs and bellies,—that is to say, every captain of a hundred footmen doth receive weekly on every Saturday his full entertainment of 28s., in like case every lieutenant 14s., every ensign 7s., our sergeant, surgeon, drum, and fife 5s., and every common soldier 3s., to be delivered to all by the pole weekly; to the four last lower officers 2s. weekly, and for every common soldier 20d. weekly, is to be answered to the full value thereof in good apparel, of different kinds, part for winter and part for summer. The apparel for an officer in winter is,—a cassock of broad cloth with bays, and trimmed with silk lace, 27s. 7d.; a doublet of canvas with silk buttons, and lined with white linen, 14s. 5d.; two shirts and two bands, 9s. 6d.; three pair of kersey stockings, at 2s. 4d. per pair; three pair of shoes of neat's leather, 2s. 4d. per pair; one pair of Venetians (a sort of long trousers), of broad Kentish cloth, with silver lace, 15s. 4d. In summer, two shirts, two pair of shoes, one pair of stockings, a felt hat and band. Apparel for a common soldier in winter:—a cassock of Kentish broad cloth, lined with cotton, and trimmed with buttons and

XIX

A.D. 1558-1603.

loops, 17s. 6d.; a doublet of canvass, with white linen lining, 12s. 6d.; a hat-cap, coloured, 7s.; two shirts of Osnaberg holland and bands, 8s.; three pair of neat's leather shoes, 2s. 4d. per pair; three pair of kersey stockings, 8s.; one pair of Venetians, of Kentish broad cloth, with buttons, loops, and lining of linen, 13s. 4d. In summer, two shirts of Osnaberg and two falling holland bands, two pair of shoes, one pair of stockings, a hat-cap, coloured."

JAMES I.

A.D. 1603—1625.

THE costume of the reign of James I. was little more than a continuation of the dress of the latter part of Elizabeth's reign. The increase in size of the breeches, from the quantity of stuffing, we may trace to the pusillanimous character of James. Dalzel tells us in his " Fragments of Scottish History," that this monarch had "his clothing made large, and even the doublets quilted for fear of stilettoes; his breeches in great plaits and full stuffed." In a MS. in the Harleian library, is the following description of the dress of the famous George Villiers, Duke of Buckingham, the favourite of James I. :—" It was common with him, at any ordinary dancing, to have his clothes trimmed with great diamond buttons, and to have diamond hatbands, cockades, and earings; to be yoked with great and manifold knots of pearl, in short, to be manacled, fettered, and imprisoned in jewels; insomuch, that at his going over to Paris in 1625, he had twenty-seven suits of clothes made the richest that embroidery, lace, silk, velvet, gold, and gems could contribute; one of which was a white uncut velvet, set all over, both suit and cloak, with diamonds, valued at fourteen thousand pounds, besides a great feather stuck all over with diamonds, as were also his sword, girdle, hatband, and spurs."

The hat worn by the knights of the Garter at this time was high-crowned, and feathers having been latterly neglected, were re-introduced in the tenth year of this reign. Some variation appears also in the colour of the mantle of foreign princes; that sent to Frederick, Duke of Wurtemberg, in the fourth year of his reign, was purple and violet mixed.

James is stated to have remarked of armour, "that it was an excellent invention, for it not only saved the life of the wearer, but prevented his hurting anybody else." The increasing use of fire-arms, combined with other causes, brought armour into disrepute, and before the close of this reign, that of the heaviest cavalry terminated at the knees.

In Plate XX. James I. is represented in the great, round, abominable breeches, tapering down to the knees; this was his hawking dress, of which sport he was fond: the entire dress was slashed all over, and it is probable that he wore stays, which was not uncommon at this period. His ugly hat was of the newest and most approved fashion, with a small feather at the side. Henry, Prince of Wales, is also pourtrayed; his armour reaches only to the waist. The gallic hosen are worn and fastened to the doublet just above the tabs by innumerable points. This very promising young man died in his nineteenth year: he was very fond of the pike exercise. His page attends him with his helmet. The fourth figure is a soldier armed with a caliver, who has no armour, but an iron morion on his head; the caliver was different from the arquebus, being of greater calibre, but it was lighter than a musket, and was fired without a rest. The intercourse with Spain changed the name of lancer into cavalier. The infantry consisted of pikemen and musketeers: the caliver came greatly into use, and ultimately superseded the long fire-arm altogether.

A military treatise, published in 1619 by a gentleman of the name of Edward Davis, tells us "that a soldier must either accustom himself to bear a piece or a pike: if he bear a piece, then must he first learn to hold the same; to accommodate his match between the two foremost fingers and his thombe, and to plant the great end on his breast with a gallant soldier-like grace. His flaske and touch-box must keep his

XX.

A.D. 1608-1625.

powder, his purse and mouth his bullets; in skirmish his left hand must hold his match and piece, and the right hand use the office of charging and discharging."

To the rest for the musket or matchlock was added, in this reign, a long rapier blade for the defence of the soldier when he had discharged his piece; it was called the swynes feather, "hogs'-bristle," and sometimes the Swedish feather, having, perhaps, been a Swedish invention. The butt-end of the pistol in this reign became elongated.

A military treatise, written in 1619, already referred to, gives long directions as to the use of the various arms of that period: amongst others, it is observed, "so some bring in a custom of too much curiositie in arming hargabusiers, for besides a piece, flaske, tutch-box, rapier and dagger, they loade them with a heavy shirt of male, and a barganet; so that by the time they have marched ten or twelve English miles, they are more apt to rest than ready to fight, whereby the enterprise they go upon, which requires celerity, shall become frustrate by reason of the stay made in refreshing themselves, or else they are in danger to be repulsed, for want of lustinesse, breath, and agilitie,"—an excellent observation on overloading the soldier.

CHARLES I.

A.D. 1625—1649.

THE costume of this reign has been deemed the most elegant and picturesque that has been adopted in England; and it never can be forgotten as long as Vandyke's paintings last; the habit of the time is consequently called Vandyke dress. This picturesque habit was introduced about the middle of this reign: at the commencement, the fashions of his father's reign were preserved, and there was scarcely a nation in Europe that had not contributed to them.

In Ben Jonson's Comedy of "The New Inn," acted in 1629, a beau observes:—

> "I would put on
> The Savoy chain about my neck, the ruff,
> The cuffs of Flanders, then the Naples hat
> With the Rome hatband, and the Florentine agate,
> The Milan sword, the cloak of Geneva set
> With Brabant buttons; all my given pieces.
> My gloves the natives of Madrid, &c. &c."

And in his "Tale of a Tub," a later performance, mention is made of "long sawsedge hose, and breeches pinned up like pudding bags;" and long breeches, in imitation of the Dutch fashion, are said to have been worn—and by Charles himself.

At the commencement of the civil war, when the royalist party began to be denominated cavaliers, and the republicans roundheads, the costume of England was as divided as its opinions; but the dress of the cavalier was gallant and picturesque in the extreme: it consisted of a doublet of silk, satin, or velvet, with large loose sleeves slashed up the front, the collar covered by a falling band of the richest point lace, with that peculiar edge now called Vandyke: a short cloak was worn carelessly on one shoulder. The long breeches, fringed or pointed, nearly met the top of the wide boots, which were also ruffled with lace or lawn. A broad-leafed Flemish beaver hat, with a rich hatband and plume of feathers, was set on one side of the head, and a Spanish rapier hung from a most magnificent baldrick, or sword-belt, worn over the right shoulder. The doublet of silk or velvet was frequently exchanged in these troublous times for a buff coat richly laced, and encircled by a broad silk or satin scarf tied in a large bow either behind or over the hip. In some instances a buff jerkin without sleeves was worn over the doublet. In the twelfth year of this reign was restored the mantle of the order of the Garter to its original colour, a rich celestial blue, and it was so worn on the installation of the Prince of Wales; the surcoat and humerale remained crimson; the hat was black velvet, as before: previous to this the knights had been ordered to wear the badge (the cross surrounded

XXI.

A.D. 1625 — 1649.

by the garter) on their daily dress. In 1629 it was formed into a star, by surrounding it with rays, as it is at present. The beard was worn very peaked, with upturned moustaches, and the hair very long.

At this period armour being considered very cumbrous, was beginning to be left off; many noblemen and officers contented themselves with a cuirass over a buff coat; but the heavy cavalry were more heavily armed, and the pikemen and musketeers were armed with helmets, back and breastplates, with tassets. The large boot was worn by many, and a large hat by some (see Plate XXI.). Dragoons, first raised in France in the year 1600, by the Marshal de Brisac, were now part of our English army, and wore at this time a buff coat with deep skirts, and an open head-piece with cheeks. According to a treatise published at Cambridge, called "Militaire Instructions for the Cavalrie," dated 1632, we find the force divided into four classes: "the Lancier, the Cuirassier, the Harquebouse and Carbine, and the Dragone." The Lancier was to wear a close casque, or head-piece, gorget, breast and back (culiver proof), pauldrons, vambraces, two gauntlets, tassets, culassets, culets, or guarde de reins, a good sword (stiff cutting and sharp pointed), with a girdle and hanger, so fastened that he might easily draw it, a buff coat with long skirts, to wear between his armour and his clothes; his lance to be eighteen feet long, with a thong of leather to fasten it round the right arm; one if not two pistols of sufficient bore and length, a flask, cartouch-box, and all appurtenances fitting. These men were therefore heavily armed. The Cuirassier was to be similarly armed, with two pistols hanging at his saddle-bow, a sword, stiff and sharp pointed, like the Lancier: he is also to wear a scarf, the only sign of uniform at the time, when the royal troops and Cromwell's were dressed so much alike; for though red was the royal colour, it was retained by many of Cromwell's troops. The Harquebusier, "by the late orders rendered in by the council of war," is to wear, besides a good buff coat, a back and breastplate, like the cuirassier, more than pistol proof, a head-piece, &c., a arquebus two feet and a half long, hung on a belt by a swivel, a flask, a touch-box, and pistols. The Carbineer is to have a good buff coat, a carbine or petronel, hanging as the arquebus, a sword, girdle and hangers, a flask, and a touch-box. The Dragone, we are told, is of two kinds, pike and musket: the pike is to have a thong of leather about the middle of it for the convenience of carrying. The Musketeer is to have a strap fastened to the stock of the piece, almost from the one end to the other, by which, being on horseback, he hangeth it at his back, keeping his burning match and bridle in the left hand. In 1645 arquebusiers were accounted the second sort of cavalry, and wore triple-barred helmets (see No. 8, Plate XXIV.), cuirasses, with guard de reins, pauldrons, and vambraces. At the same time the dragoons changed their muskets for the shorter piece called the dragon, from whence they had derived their name abroad; and in 1649 they carried the caliver. The pot helmet, or open head-piece, with cheeks (see No. 6, Plate XXIV.), the single and triple-barred helmet worn by the dragoons and arquebusiers of this period (Nos. 7 and 8, Plate XXIV.), are taken from drawings made from those at Goodrich Court. The modern firelock was invented about this time, and the improvement was suggested from a fire-arm called snaphansier, from its being invented by a set of Dutch marauders called *snaphans*, or poultry stealers, who found the light of the match betrayed them in their marauding trips, and substituted the flint and an upright movable piece of steel, in lieu of the wheel lock, which was too expensive for them. The snaphaunce was known in Elizabeth's time, but the firelock dates from about 1635. Before this invention the wheel lock was frequently called the firelock: the musket-rest and swynes feathers were abandoned at the end of the civil wars.

Great reliance was placed in the pikemen during this reign: his pike was certainly a formidable weapon, eighteen feet long. Wardle, in his "Animadversions of Warre," vol. ii. p. 90, edit. in 1639, says, "So long as the pikes stand firme, altho' the shot should be routed, yet it cannot be said the field was won, for the whole strength of an army consists in pikes." In 1625 the infantry consisted of pikemen, musketeers, those armed with calivers, and those armed with rondashes. Of these the first and last wore corslets; those with the rondashes having sometimes a close helmet, at other times an open head-piece.

Although armour was on the decline, the troops at this period were still heavily armed, for the thickness of the breastplates were expected to be bullet proof. Charles I. granted to William Drummond for the sole making and vending many warlike machines. The first was an equestrian instrument by which a single horseman should be equal to fight five or six men with common arms. The second was a new kind of spear, with which a foot soldier, besides using it as a pike, may discharge five or six guns, to be called a pike arquebus. The third was a machine of congregated muskets, by which one or two soldiers could oppose a hundred guns, called the "thundering chariot!" and many other wonderful inventions; but as none of them have been handed down to the present age, we may pronounce they were humbugs.

THE COMMONWEALTH.

A.D. 1649—1660.

The exaggerations in costume of the court of Charles I. were considerably lowered by the feelings of puritanism, and by the soberness of manners consequent on the troubles of this period. The roundheads, who obtained that name from the more worthless cavaliers, in consequence of cropping their hair closely, giving their heads a spherical appearance, were a very different people from the adherents of Charles I.: their show of plainness, though intended as a sign of innate modesty, frequently covered as much vanity as was displayed in the outward appearance of the gayest gallants. When Cromwell obtained the ascendancy, plain attire was paramount; an attention to dress never troubled the mind intent on matters of higher importance. Sir Philip Warwick describes Oliver Cromwell in the House of Parliament, before he had arrived at importance, thus:—"The first time that I ever took notice of him, was in the beginning of the Parliament held in November, 1640, when I vainly thought myself a courtly young gentleman; for we courtiers valued ourselves much upon our good clothes. I came one morning into the house well clad, and perceived a gentleman speaking whom I knew not, very ordinarily apparelled, for it was a plain cloth suit, which seemed to have been made by an ill country tailor; his linen was also plain, and not very clean; and I remember a speck or two of blood upon his little band; his hat was without a hatband; his stature was of a good size; his sword stuck close to his side."

The comely young gentlemen of this period valued themselves much upon gay clothes; and with reason, perhaps, for there was little else about many of them of any value.

The gloomy puritanism that overshadowed the land for a time, and damped the natural cheerfulness of the heart, that railed at a may-pole as a "stinking idol," and frowned down all innocent festivities as sinful! was, however, rebelled against by a few daring spirits, who would wear their hair above an inch long, and wide collars covering their shoulders; there were others who kept up cavalier fashions and festivities, and were ready to exclaim with Shakespere's Sir Toby Belch, "What, dost thou think, because thou art virtuous, there shall be no more cakes and ale?"

At a later period of Cromwell rule, long hair began to make its appearance among the clergy.

A portion of the cavalry under Charles I. were denominated cavaliers, but the term becoming offensive to the levellers of the period, they were gradually replaced by a different class of men under Cromwell, and nominated pistoliers, arquebusiers, &c. &c. The armour of the pistolier was nearly that of the cavalier, which, soon after the establishment of the protectorate, was disused, and the cuirass only worn. They were called cuirassiers, and armed with an open helmet, and a breast and backplate, under which was a buff coat: his arms were a spit sword with a sharp point, and pistols or petronels: his saddle and bit were made very strong, and the reins of the bridle guarded with an iron chain to prevent being cut. The wearing armour to the knees

XXXI.

A.D. 1649—1660.

had been continued to this time, the lance being in constant use, against which weapon strong armour was the only effectual resistance. The corslet seems also to have been laid aside in Cromwell's time, and the musket-rest was not used long after this period. The gorgets were now made much larger, and often worn alone over the buff coat. One of the figures in Plate XXII. represents the dress of Oliver Cromwell, with a large gorget over a buff coat, without a cuirass: the helmet is drawn from one he wore, a most excellent protection to the head, firm and warlike. The other figure is Robert Devereux, Earl of Essex, who commanded the parliamentary army, taken from an old and rare print: he wears a cuirass, and indulges in a large collar to his shirt, and breeches and boots rather partaking of the cavalier's fashion. At the breaking out of the civil war, the Earl of Essex issued a precept, dated November, 1643, "for stirring up all well-affected people, by benevolence, towards the raising of a company of archers for the service of the King and Parliament."

Charles I. wrote, in 1640, a military code: the Earl of Essex followed his example, and in 1643 published another for the government of the parliamentary army. Charles I. took great pains to bring about an uniformity in the fashion of armour amongst his officers and soldiers. This was a good deal disturbed during the civil wars.

The Earl of Essex, before his arrival at Worcester on September 24, 1642, addressed his army, "requesting that they might be well instructed in the necessary rudiments of war, that they may know how to fall on with discretion and retreat with care, how to maintain their order and to make good their ground." There were experienced officers during Charles I.'s time who reluctantly allowed the arquebus and musket to supersede the long-bow—Charles having twice granted a commission for enforcing the use of the bow: "and he granted a commission to William Nead and his son to teach and exercise his loving subjects in his new invention of using the pike and bow together;" one so armed was called a double-armed man.

Cromwell's troops had generally basket-hilted swords, closely resembling the Scotch, the blades being both curved and straight. The basket-hilt probably commenced in the time of James I. when gauntlets began to be disused. A pleasing description of the dress of this period is given in "Memoirs and Correspondence of Prince Rupert and the Cavaliers."

"Prince Rupert, after defeating the garrison of Rhenins, which he had wantonly provoked, resumed his march: a picturesque array, accoutred in the old chivalric fashion, with plumed helmet and bright armour, over a leathern doublet, steel cuisses to the knee, and huge gambadoes with the large knightly spur. Tall powerful horses, such as Wouvermans has left us, stepped proudly under their caparisons; and the small cornet or flag that fluttered over each troop gave a liveliness to the glaring column as it wound along the wide plains of Hanover. The few infantry belonging to the army were armed with the pike, arquebus or musket, steel cap and corslet."

The rondell or rondash, which had been revived by Prince Maurice, was disused in the early part of the reign of Charles I.; it was a shield, in the upper part of which was a horizontal aperture for vision, and on the right side in the edge, an oblique one, through which the sword was thrust. It was black, and so thick, as to resist the penetration of bullets, when not fired very near.

Although there was an affectation of despising gay dress in Oliver Cromwell's party, yet there were in the republican army many commanders who, boasting of very remote ancestry, retained the arms of their families, and bore them on pennons. They had likewise large square banners, upon which were painted devices and mottoes alluding to the principles of the cause they had undertaken to defend, and expressive of the fanatic spirit, in which they gloried. Oliver Cromwell's funeral was attended with much magnificence: there were new banners made for the occasion, the expense of which amounted to 700*l*., a good deal of money in those days.

The strength of the army in England in 1652, cavalry and infantry, was 31,519 men, exclusive of officers; and the army in Ireland amounted to nearly 20,000 : making a total standing army of more than 50,000 men. The Protector afterwards reduced it to 30,000. The foot soldiers had commonly 1s. a day; the horse 2s. 6d. per diem. Many gentlemen and younger brothers of good families enlisted in the Protector's cavalry.

CHARLES II.

A.D. 1660—1685.

THE moment Charles II. landed at Dover, in May 1660, although he could not help admiring the martial appearance of those warriors, who had defeated the adherents of his father, yet he disbanded the army. A body of life guards, consisting of two regiments, were raised; the privates of which were gentlemen who had followed the fortunes of Charles I. during the civil war; and the high privileges they obtained were continued long after the time when they ceased to be composed of the same class of men. The Duke of Albemarle recommended the arming musqueteers and dragoons with muskets having what was called sweyne's feathers, which answered the purpose of bayonets, and were carried in sheaths, so as to serve as walking-sticks, but capable of being quickly drawn out and fixed in the muzzle of the muskets. Turner says, "musket-rests were still used to ease musqueteers in discharging their guns, and in standing sentinel; but in the late expeditions in Christendom, they have been found more troublesome than helpful. A musqueteer," he adds, "in any sudden occasion, not being well able to do his duty with musket, sword, and rest, especially if he had a Swedish feather to manage with them." The same author further observes, "To the musqueteer belongs also a bandolier of leather, at which he should have hanging eleven or twelve shot of powder, a bag of ball, a primer and a cleaner; but it is thirty years," he says, "since these have been laid aside in some German armies; for it is impossible for soldiers, especially without cloaks, which is the case with some of our men, to keep these flasks, though well and strongly made, from snow and rain, which soon spoils them, and makes the powder altogether useless; besides the noise they make betray those who carry them, in all surprisals, onslaughts, and sudden enterprises."

Plate XXIII. represents a cuirassier, or officer of life guards, an arquebusier and a musqueteer, who is armed with a musket, rest, and bandoliers. The sweyne feather rest and sweyne feather were soon laid aside, and soldiers armed with daggers, stuck them into the muzzles of their pieces. This was the origin of the bayonet, which was invented at Bayonne, and called by the French " bayonets à manche," first introduced into their army in 1671: they were made with plain handles, to fix in the muzzle. Turner mentions that improvements in the German armies had taken place thirty years before the heavy appointments, so disadvantageous to a soldier, had been thrown aside in our army. This great inattention to improvement is characteristic of our system, and still exists at head-quarters. Many contrivances were tried to protect the musqueteer, after discharging his piece, from the attack of cavalry, before the present bayonet was invented; and nearly three hundred years elapsed after the invention of hand guns before the contrivance of cartridges occurred.

Bandoliers were still worn in 1670, but had been gradually growing into disuse. Lord Orrery recommended cartridge boxes of tin, on the principle of the old pattern of Elizabeth's time. The boots of this period were of that large kind called gambado, having very large tops to them, which were introduced to prevent the leg from being crushed in a charge. The large hat with feathers was now in fashion as a military head dress: down went the crown, and up went the brims at the sides; a row of feathers were placed round it, in lieu of the chivalric plume, and this led to the cocked hat of the eighteenth century. The irresistible fashion of the Court was not to be withstood: the warlike helmet was given up for the insecure hat; but the conviction of the want of protection to the head, in such a dress, against the sabre, led to the invention of a small steel cap, which was sown inside the crown of the

XXIII

A D 1660-1685.

hat. Lord Orrery, in his work called the "Art of War," published in 1677, writes, "Our foot are generally two-thirds shot, and one-third pikes. In the last battle we fought in Ireland, 1200 of the enemy's pikes charged and routed our horse. The pike ought to be sixteen feet long; the men three feet apart and five deep make an impervious body: he should be armed with back and breast pieces, pott and taces." Munro is very enthusiastic in praise of this Tipperary weapon, "that niver missed fire;" he adds, "this much in briefe for the pike, the most honorable of all weapons; and my choice in the day of battel, leading a storm, or entering a breech, with a light breastplate and good head-piece, being seconded with good fellows, I would only ask a half pike to enter with." The arquebus was at this time a matchlock, or heavy musket used in action with a rest which was trailed, when moving from the wrist.

No doubt Charles II. disbanded Oliver Cromwell's experienced and gallant army with reluctance: fears of infidelity, however, overruled other feelings, and the advantage of retaining a military force of his own formation to support his recently restored authority, officered by known royalists, induced him to raise the following regiments:—the life guards in the year 1661; the horse guards blue, or Oxford blues, in the same year, so called from being raised by the Earl of Oxford. The Coldstream foot guards date their formation from 1660, when two regiments were added to the one raised about ten years previously by General Monk, at Coldstream on the Scotch border. The first royal Scots were brought over from France at the Restoration; the second Queen's, raised in 1661; the third, or Buffs, so called from their accoutrements being composed of buffalo leather, embodied in 1665; the North British fusileers, now the twenty-first foot, raised in 1678, and so called from their carrying the fusil, a firelock lighter than the musket, invented in France in 1630; the fourth, or King's Own, raised in 1680. The whole force was reviewed on Putney Heath on the 1st of October, 1684, amounting to 4000 men, commanded in chief by the Earl of Craven. In the thirteenth year of this reign the army was ordered to be thus armed:—the defensive arms of cavalry, a back, breast, and pott, the breast and pott to be pistol-proof; the offensive arms, a sword and a case of pistols, the barrels whereof not to be under fourteen inches in length; the furniture of the horse to be a great saddle, with burrs and straps, also with straps to affix the holsters unto, a bit and bridle, with a pectoral and crupper. In the foot, the musqueteer to have a musket, the barrel whereof not to be less than three feet in length, and the gauge of the bore not to be less than twelve bullets to the pound; a collar of bandoliers, with a sword. A pikeman, whose pike is to be made of ash, not under sixteen feet long, the head and foot included, with a back, breast, head-piece, and sword. The tallest and strongest men were generally selected for the pike, and their pay was somewhat greater than that of a musqueteer. Officers at this time often wore no other armour than a large gorget, which nearly served the purpose of a breastplate.

Archery was continued as an amusement, the king himself sometimes attending exhibitions of shooting. But in a pamphlet, written in 1664, giving an account of the success of the Marquis of Montrose against the Scots, bowmen are repeatedly mentioned as having been engaged in that battle. The grenadiers of the Highland regiments, indeed as late as the time of William III., when recruiting, wore the old red bonnet, and carried bows and arrows. Hume, in his account of the Rebellion of 1648, mentions that a clergyman going to perform divine service held a bow in his hand, and carried the arrows in a silk sash tied round his waist. The Highland bow was short, and not very powerful. About this period silk armour was invented, it was said, to protect the Protestants from assassination by the Papists. The inconvenient weight of breast and back-plates of steel induced this invention: a doublet and breeches of quilted silk was so closely stitched, and of such thickness as to be proof against bullet or steel, and a thick bonnet of the same materials, with ear-flaps attached to it, protected the head; the whole was of a dusky orange colour. The Honourable Roger North speaking of it, says, "there were abundance of those silken back, breast, and potts made and sold, that were pretended to be pistol-proof, in which any man dressed was as safe as in a house, for

XXIIII.

1646.

it was impossible any one could strike at him for laughing, so ridiculous was the figure, as they say, of hogs in armour."

A cuirassier's armour in this reign cost 4*l*. 10*s*., a footman's armour 1*l*. 2*s*. Rapid changes in dress were now taking place: the costume of Charles I. was on the decline, the people were tired of the dull apparel of the stern Puritans, and, on the restoration of the House of Stuart, plunged into all the excesses of the French, guided by bad taste. Armour was nearly disused; and the square coat, cocked hat, full-bottomed wig, and jack-boots, and all the fashions of the Court of Louis XIV. of France, found their way to England; and the servile imitators of the " grande monarque," instituted that detestable monstrosity, the periwig. The costume of the Knights of the Garter became in this reign exactly what it is at present. Before leaving the House of Stuart, it may not be considered out of place to introduce one of the gayest of the Parliamentary generals, and a dandy or exquisite of that period, evidently not a Puritan.

Plate XXIV. represents Ferdinand Lord Fairfax, the father of the more celebrated parliamentary general, who also served in the same cause, and was appointed general for the county of York. He has on a cuirass over a highly ornamented buff coat, his boot-tops are turned down to show the inside ornamented with lace, they turn up over the knee when required. The second figure in this plate, is a representation of a first-rate exquisite, copied from a rare print of 1646, styled "The picture of an English anticke, with a list of his ridiculous habits and apish gestures." His face is spotted with patches; he has two love-locks hanging on his breast, tied at the ends with silk riband in bows; his breeches have many dozen points at the knees, and bunches of riband of several colours above them; his boot-tops very large, fringed with lace, and turned down as low as his spurs, which gingled like bells as he walked, the feet of the boots two inches too long; he carried a stick, which he played with as he straddled along the streets singing.

PLATE XXV.

Nos. 1, 2, and 3, are morions of the time of Elizabeth.

No. 4, a Bourginet of the time of James I. No. 6, is a morion of the same period.

No. 5, is a curious cap made of iron bars, covered with stout black leather, of the time of the Commonwealth, in possession of F. Popham, Esq., of Littlecote.

Nos. 7, 8, and 9, are helmets of the time of Charles I. and the Commonwealth.

No. 10, is a helmet which is said to have belonged to Oliver Cromwell.

No. 11, this helmet is supposed to have belonged to the Duke of Monmouth, who was beheaded July 15, 1685.

XXV

A.D. 1558—1685.

JAMES II.

A.D. 1685—1688.

It is said that Charles II., when a little boy, had a beautiful head of hair, which hung in long waving curls upon his shoulders, and the courtiers, out of compliment to their young sovereign, had heads of false hair made to imitate his natural locks, which obtained the name of perukes. When the king grew up, he returned the compliment by adopting the article himself, and the peruke was speedily placed upon the heads and shoulders of all the gentlemen of England. This absurd and most objectionable piece of art was continued by the courtiers of James II.; and William III. indulged in a more monstrous wig than any which had preceded it. Had this ridiculous fashion remained merely with the Court, it would have been of little importance; but military men followed the practice, and introduced into the army a head-dress, in every respect grotesque and inconvenient, which run through the reigns of William III., of Anne, of George I. and II., in all kinds of exaggerated shapes. What sensible man of the present day will not express surprise that the greatest generals of that period (our Marlborough included) should have made such tom-fools of themselves? The beaux of this time combed their perukes publicly, and had large combs of ivory, or tortoise-shell, curiously chased and ornamented, which were used at Court, in the Mall, and in the boxes of the theatre. A gallant combed his peruke while in conversation, or flirtation, with the same air with which a modern exquisite twirls his moustaches. The helmet was now seldom worn; the hat, with the brims turned up, ornamented with feathers all round, and placed on the top of a full flowing wig, was a most ridiculous contrast to a steel cuirass. It was a wonderful change from the dress of the Puritans, who thought they could not cut their hair too short; for now old and young, civil or military, not being able to make their hair grow long enough by natural means, in despair shaved their heads and wore wigs.

Plate XXVI. represents the Duke of Monmouth and Lord Grey, who commanded the duke's horse at the battle of Sedgmoor. History states that the battle at one time was somewhat in favour of Monmouth, but that the general commanding the horse wanted that essential for a soldier,—courage! Lord Grey, in the drawing, is leaving the fight at the best pace a tired horse could go, taking his hat off to the duke on passing him. Monmouth paused for some little time, when, seeing the battle was lost, he hopelessly put spurs to his horse, and riding till he could carry him no longer, dismounted, changed his dress with a peasant, and hid himself in a ditch, where he was found in a very distressed state, bodily and mentally. He was taken to King James, and on the 15th July, 1685, was beheaded. There was a hat turned up at the sides called the Monmouth cock, whether in derision or not history does not inform us.

Carabineers, so called from the fire-arm they carried, were raised in this reign, and formed into regiments in the following one: they wore breast and back plates, and iron skull-caps sewn in the crowns of cocked hats; they were armed with swords, and carried pistols in holsters; the carbine slung behind by a belt and swivel. James added to the British cavalry the first King's dragoon guards in 1685, and the second dragoon guards in the same year; they were trained to act either on foot or horseback, the men having firelocks and bayonets, in addition to swords and pistols. To the infantry were added the fifth and seventh regiments (the latter called the Royal fusiliers) both embodied in 1685, and the twenty-third, or Welsh fusiliers, in 1688. The prices of clothing for the army in 1678 were: a footman 2*l*. 13*s*., dragoon 6*l*. 10*s*., horse 9*l*., horse grenadiers 8*l*. Charles, at the beginning of his reign, had nearly 5000 men of guards and garrison; at the end of his reign the number was increased to nearly 8000. James, at Monmouth's rebellion, had almost 15,000 troops; and when the Prince of Orange landed, no less than 30,000 regular troops in England.

XXVI.

1685 — 1688.

WILLIAM AND MARY.

A.D. 1688—1702.

The reign of James II. terminated prematurely, but the perukes remained in fashion long after he had fled the kingdom. In William's reign they were in full force; and though there was much written and spoken against them, the tide of fashion was too strong for all opposition: indeed they increased in magnitude even on the shoulders of military men. The church and law having adopted them, it was supposed there must be wisdom in a wig. The church in our days has thrown them aside, but the law still indulges in them, in powdered magnificence. In William III.'s reign there lived a witty perruquier who, anxious to uphold even the utility of the peruke, hired a sign-painter, to paint Absalom hanging by his hair to a tree, and David weeping beneath as he exclaimed,

> "O Absalom! O Absalom!
> O Absalom my son!
> If thou hadst worn a periwig
> Thou hadst not been undone."

Marines were embodied in this reign, and put on the establishment of the navy, and afterwards disbanded; they were again raised in Queen Anne's time, formed into six regiments, and dressed as soldiers. The heavy cavalry continued to be armed with backs, breasts, and potts to the time of the Prince of Orange's landing at Torbay, November 5, 1688, when the royal regiment of horse guards blue was ordered to march from Winchester to Salisbury, and to leave their armour in charge of the Mayor of Winchester. This order may have originated in a wish to favour the Prince of Orange, or from cuirasses being considered heavy and useless. Whether they resumed them afterwards does not appear; but in 1794 this regiment was supplied with breastplates, which had been used in previous campaigns in the Netherlands, they were considered so cumbersome and inconvenient as to be given up, and never resumed till the coronation of George IV., when the household brigade appeared in bright steel cuirasses and helmets, and have worn them ever since. The blues at the same time changed the buff belts for white ones.

Half-pay for officers was instituted in this reign. Most of the troops were now armed with muskets or firelocks in the place of matchlocks. The musqueteers fired three deep, the front rank kneeling; the grenadiers practised the grenade exercise. When a regiment of cavalry was drawn up for review (according to Markham), the files were six deep. The horse grenadiers were armed with muskets and grenades, and were used dismounted as well as mounted. The exercise of the dragoons was nearly the same. The bayonet was still a dagger; but the ring added to the guard, at first for defence, was brought into great use at this time on the Continent. In one of the campaigns in Flanders, a French regiment advanced against the British twenty-fifth with bayonets fixed by a ring over the muzzles of their muskets; Lieutenant-colonel Maxwell, who commanded the regiment, ordered his men to screw their bayonets into the muzzles of their muskets, thinking the French intended to charge; when suddenly they poured in a heavy fire, to the astonishment of the British, who could not understand how it was possible to fire with fixed bayonets: however, they recovered themselves, charged, and drove the enemy out of the line. Our eyes were then opened, and, slow as we are at military inventions, we can avail ourselves of those of other nations, after having suffered from them. The socket bayonet was speedily adopted, and displaced the pike entirely.

Plate XXVII. represents the Duke of Schomberg and the French General Caillemot in William's service, who were killed at the battle of the Boyne: the former was in his eighty-second year. The drawing of the Duke of Schomberg is copied from a portrait by Sir G. Kneller. Portrait painters of that period always dressed their subjects in armour, if they were military men; it is, however, doubtful if the duke wore such complete armour on the day of the battle as he is here represented

XXVII

1688 — 1701

in: no doubt the drawing of the monstrous peruke is correct. At the battle of the Boyne, every man of William's army wore a sprig fastened in his hat, to distinguish him from James's men, who wore bits of white paper.

In 1695, the coats and breeches of the sergeants and soldiers were of a grey colour; the coats of the drummers were purple, with grey breeches; they were likewise distinguished by badges. James is said to have worn, at the battle of the Boyne, a cuirass which was given him by Louis XIV. on his leaving France for the vain attempt to recover the throne of England. The French king, on presenting it, said—"The best thing I can wish you is, that I may never see you again." This wish, however, was not realized: after James's unsuccessful campaign in Ireland, he returned to France, and died at St. Germains on the 16th September, 1701.

William III. died on the 8th March, 1702.

QUEEN ANNE.

A.D. 1702—1714.

ALL chivalric costume ended in this reign; the sword alone continued to be worn at court, and sometimes in full dress. Square-cut coats and long-flapped waistcoats, with large pockets to both; the stockings drawn up over the knee so high as to hide the breeches, but gartered below it; large hanging cuffs and laced ruffles; the skirts of the coats stiffened out with wire or buckram, from between which peeped the hilt of the sword, deprived of the broad and splendid belt from which it swung in the preceding reigns; blue or scarlet stockings with gold or silver clocks; lace neckcloths; square-toed, short-quartered shoes, with high heels and small buckles; very long and formally-curled perukes, black riding wigs, long wigs, and night-cap wigs; small three-cornered hats laced with gold or silver galloon, and sometimes trimmed with feathers, composed the habit of the noblemen and gentlemen. The accession of a queen to the throne of England was not likely to cause any alteration in the costume of gentlemen. Anne was naturally of a retiring disposition, and entirely in the power of Sarah, Duchess of Marlborough, who was so much given to state intrigue as not to care about costume; yet the queen was strict regarding the dress of those about the court, and would remark whether a periwig or the lining of a coat was appropriate. She once sent for Lord Bolingbroke in haste, who immediately attended in a Ramilies tie instead of a full-bottomed wig, at which she was greatly offended.

Armour for infantry being now completely thrown aside, the foot wore an easy scarlet coat with facings, a cocked hat, breeches, and long black gaiters coming up above the knee, with a strap below the knee to keep them up. The cavalry also wore the cocked hat, and large boots; the cuirass was almost given up. Some officers wore a wide-brimmed hat, turned up on two sides, and feathers. Fashions arose from leaders of ton and in commemoration of some public event. The famous battle of Ramilies, for instance, introduced the Ramilies cock of the hat; and the hair was formed into a tail, with a bow at the top, called a Ramilies tie.

In Plate XXVIII. is represented the costume of the soldiers who fought in Marlborough's wars, three foot and three horsemen; the foot soldier in the foreground with his back turned to us shows the Ramilies tail. One of the mounted men has a wide-brimmed hat and plumes, with the flowing wig, which was still worn by officers of rank. Tying the hair is said to have been first introduced by the noted Lord Bolingbroke.

There was a punishment in the army which remained in force till this reign, when it was abolished; it was the only corporal punishment which could be inflicted on an officer; that of boring the tongue with a hot iron for blasphemy.

The cocked hat was worn by all persons of any rank in society: and we learn from the "Spectator" that one John Sly prepared hats for all kinds of heads of persons who made some figure in the realm of Great

XXVIII

1701 — 1714.

XIX.

1714 — 1760.

Britain, with cocks significant of their powers and faculties. His hats for men of the faculties of law or physic did but just turn up to give a little life to their sagacity; his military hats glared full in the face to increase the bravery of appearance.

GEORGE I. AND GEORGE II.

A.D. 1714—1760.

THERE were no very great alterations in the character of dress during these reigns; to the catalogue of wigs we find added the tie-wig and the bob-wig, the latter worn sometimes without powder. The Ramilies tail was followed by the pig-tail, which was adopted about the year 1745; and some young men wore their own hair dressed and profusely powdered. The military wore powder with the head well larded; at one time long tails, at another a thick tail clubbed, as it was called, which was turning it up, leaving a great knob below, and securing it with a leather strap.

Plate XXIX. represents a heavy and light dragoon and two guardsmen of this period, about the time of Wolfe's death, 1759, at the taking of Quebec. The ridiculous cap worn by the guardsman is of German origin, and was in general use as a grenadier's cap at this time. It appears in many of Hogarth's prints—the March to Finchley and others. The heavy dragoon retains the cocked hat laced, and the large boots, though something smaller than the Dutch boot introduced by William; he has an aiguillette on his shoulder, which was at that time worn by our troopers, the most inconvenient and unmilitary ornament a soldier can wear, fit only for a footman. The figure on the left of the print is a man of the fifteenth light dragoons, whose cap though not really handsome is tolerably well shaped, not much overweighted at top, and is a good protection to the head; on the front of the cap is written "Meribimur," round the front edge is inscribed "Five battalions of French defeated and taken by this regiment, with their colors, and nine pieces of cannon, on the plains of Emsdorf, July 16th, 1760." The fifteenth hussars still retain "Emsdorf" on their appointments, as a record of this gallant exploit. The boots are of a lighter description, with leather breeches, and rather a becoming scarlet coat: the dress is not a bad one.

George II. reviewed the guards in 1727, habited in grey cloth faced with purple, with a purple feather in his hat; and the three eldest princesses went to Richmond in riding-habits, with hats, and feathers, and periwigs.

In the year 1729 the dragoons wore a shoulder-belt for the pouch, a waist-belt for the sword, with a place to receive a bayonet, and sling for the carbine or pistol. In 1736 the cloaks of the troopers were faced with the livery of the regiment, and all the men had laced hats.

In 1744 a private soldier of foot required two yards and three-eighths of cloth for his coat, a grenadier two yards and a half. The expenses of the soldier's dress is fully detailed in "Grove's History of the English Army."

In the reign of George I., on one of the anniversaries of the Restoration, great tumults arose, the guards became mutinous on receiving, as part of their clothing, some remarkably coarse linen. The soldiers threw some of their shirts into the king's and duke's gardens in the park, saying they were "Hanover shirts;" and there being foundation for the grievance, the linen was publicly burnt at Whitehall, and the Duke of Marlborough made a conciliatory speech on the occasion to the first regiment. These regiments behaved nobly afterwards at the battle of Fontenoy. Their uniform, as now, was royal—scarlet and blue facings.

The regiment of artillery was formed in George II.'s reign; their uniform blue faced with red. The officers wore red waistcoat and breeches.

In the year 1727 Parliament voted that the navy should consist of twenty thousand men, and the army of twenty-six thousand.

The dressing of the hair and the cock of the hat was very much thought of during this reign, not only by the military, but by civilians. There is a ridiculous letter in the "Rambler," dated 1751, from a young gentleman, who writes, "that his mother would rather follow him to the grave than see him sneak about with dirty shoes, and blotted fingers, hair unpowdered, and a hat uncocked;" and in 1753 the "Adventurer" contains a description of the gradual metamorphosis of a greenhorn into a blood. "I cut off my hair and procured a brown bob periwig of Wilding, of the same colour, with a single row of curls just round the bottom, which I wore very nicely combed and without powder: my hat, which had been cocked with great exactness in an equilateral triangle, I discarded, and purchased one of a more fashionable size, the fore corner of which projected near two inches further than those on each side, and was moulded into the shape of a spout." The fashion, however, soon changed, the fore corner "was no longer the longest, like a spout, but like the corner of a minced pye." This latter fashion was succeeded by a larger cocked hat imported from Germany, and distinguished by the name of Kevenhuller.

GEORGE III.

A.D. 1760—1820, including the Regency of 10 years.

HATS and wigs are the remarkable parts of the costume of the early part of this reign. We are told that hats were worn on an average six inches and three-fifths broad in the brim and cocked, between the quaker and the Kevenhuller: some had their hats open before, like a church spout, or the scales they weighed flour in; some wore them sharper, like the nose of a greyhound; and the mood of the wearer's mind was to be distinguished by the cock of his hat. The military and the mercantile cock were very different. The beaux of St. James's wore their hats differently from those of Moorfields, who wore them diagonally over the left eye. The gawkies wore the corner which should come over the forehead pointed into the air; others did not above half cover their heads with their hats. A hat edged with gold binding distinguished "the brothers of the turf." In 1770 the Nivernois hat was the rage; it was exceedingly small, and the flaps fastened up to the shallow crown by hooks and eyes, the crown being seen above them. Gold-laced hats were again in fashion in 1775; and in 1778 were adopted by many to give a military appearance, and to escape press-gangs, which were remarkably active in that year. The revolution in France in 1789 caused the downfall of cocked hats, except for the military: they were laughed out of fashion in England by the nickname of an "Egham, Staines, and Windsor," being compared to the triangular direction-post which pointed to those three places. The old cocked hat is still worn, with the old-fashioned dress, by the Greenwich and Chelsea pensioners.

The wig, also, felt the influence of the French revolution; it had been gradually diminishing in size during the last half century, and the practice of frizzing, plastering, and powdering the hair till it was uglier than a wig came into fashion. The poor soldiers, who have always been compelled to follow fashion, however ugly, and unfit for military purposes, were not yet released from the torture of hair-dressing: stiff curls were worn on each side, and a long tail behind, the whole plastered and powdered. The officers, perhaps, could afford pomatum; but the privates used the end of a tallow candle to keep this wonderful head-dress in regulation order. The army was tormented with this preposterous and most unwarlike method of dressing the hair, varying from club-tails to maccaroni tails and pig-tails. In the year 1804 the tails were ridiculous in length, an order was issued to reduce them to seven inches; and in 1808 the whole tails of the army were ordered to be cut off, an order which was obeyed with the greatest alacrity. The event is commemorated in that droll satire, the "Rejected Addresses:"

> "Though humbled Gallia scoff,
> God bless their pigtails though they're now cut off."

x x x

1785.

The day after the order to dock the tails arrived, a counter-order came; it was too late, the tails were gone.

To such an excess was this carried during the command of the late Duke of Kent at Gibraltar, that when a field-day was ordered, there not being sufficient barbers in the garrison to attend all the officers in the morning, the seniors claimed the privilege of their rank; the juniors consequently were obliged to have their heads dressed the night before; and to preserve the beauty of this artistic arrangement, pomatumed, powdered, curled, and clubbed, these poor fellows were obliged to sleep on their faces! It is said, that in the adjutant's office of each regiment there was kept a pattern of the correct curls, to which the barbers could refer.

The dragoon regiments raised in the reign of George II. were very heavily appointed. They wore a laced cocked hat, a very square-tailed coat, large jack boots, and an aiguillette on the shoulder. Plate XXX. represents an officer of the fourth dragoons, dressed according to an order dated in 1784, by which the officers and men were to wear epaulettes instead of aiguillettes; the jacked leather boots were replaced by others of a lighter description: the colour of the waistcoat and breeches was changed from green to white, they having hitherto been of the same colour as the facings. Directions were given for the regiment to be mounted on long-tailed horses; the tails of the horses having formerly been cut as close as possible, leaving only a stump. This order was general for the dragoons. The private's dress was the same in form as the officers, but white tape was used in the place of the silver lace. They still suffered from powdered, greased, curled, and clubbed hair.

When first regiments were raised, they went by the name of their colonels. The fourth was numbered with many others in 1751, although raised in 1685, and called "Princess Anne of Denmark's dragoons;" but it was best known at different periods up to 1751 as Berkley's, Fitzharding's, Essex's, Temple's, Evans's, and Riche's dragoons.

In 1755, a light troop was added to each regiment of dragoons, which, in the following year, consisted of one hundred men and officers.

It was to perform similar duties with those of the light companies attached to regiments of infantry. In 1763 the light troop was disbanded, and eight men of each of the six troops were equipped as light dragoons, and mounted on smaller horses for skirmishing and other light services. In 1779, the men equipped as light dragoons of the first and second dragoon guards, and the fourth dragoons, were formed into one regiment, and numbered the nineteenth light dragoons.

The two first regiments of light dragoons were raised in 1759, and were called by the names of their commanders. The gallant conduct of the fifteenth at Emsdorf has already been recorded; the sixteenth, in 1762, equally distinguished itself in Portugal under its first commander, Brigadier-General Burgoyne.

The king reviewed both regiments in brigade on Wimbledon Common, on the twentieth of May, 1766, and commanded that the fifteenth should be styled the King's and the sixteenth the Queen's light dragoons. The uniform in 1768 was a helmet with horse-hair crest, scarlet coat, blue half lappels, and the sleeves turned up with blue, the buttons of white metal two and two; a blue cloth epaulette on each shoulder, with a narrow worsted fringe; waistcoat and breeches white; boots reaching to the knee; the cloak scarlet, with a white lining and a blue cape. The trumpeters wore hats with scarlet feathers, and scarlet coats with yellow lace. In 1784 the colour was changed from scarlet to blue, and a jacket substituted for the coat, with the collar and cuffs the colour of the facings of the regiment. The front of the jacket was laced with a white cord: the breeches were white leather, worn with high boots. The helmet was changed in shape. Tight leather pantaloons and hessian boots were afterwards introduced, and the spur was fixed into the heel; but these did not long remain in fashion.

Plate XXXI. represents His Majesty George III. in the dress of a general officer of the year 1805, attended by an officer of heavy and light dragoons. The sentry presenting arms is a fusilier, whose dress is a scarlet coat, blue facings, white breeches and waistcoat, black gaiters up to the knee, a bearskin cap with a brass plate in front. Fusiliers

XXXI

1805.

XXXII

1811.

had the privilege of wearing a bearskin cap! The hat of the king is of extraordinary size, larger than a Kevenhuller, with a black cockade, and a preposterous feather.

Early in this reign, the pointed grenadier cap, represented in Plate XXIX., was exchanged for a large bearskin cap, which has been increasing in size ever since.

In the time of George II., officers wore the sash over the shoulder: in this reign it was worn round the waist. Officers of cavalry were ordered to tie it on the right side, those of the infantry on the left. Infantry of the line in 1808 wore a felt cap, with a brass plate in the front: they had a jacket with short skirts, white breeches, and long black gaiters. The officers retained the cocked hat; but soon afterwards, during the Peninsular war, they wore the same description of cap as the privates. Trousers and short gaiters were adopted, being much more convenient than breeches and long gaiters, which had fourteen or fifteen buttons on each leg.

In Egypt, the officers of infantry, and those on the staff with Abercromby's army, wore a hat of the common kind, with a feather in it. Our marines used to wear a beaver hat with the sides looped up; a head-dress well suited to their duties.

A large force went to Portugal in 1808 and 1809. The heavy cavalry were dressed as represented in Plate XXXII., in which two of the old heavies (as they were called) are portrayed, one belonging to the third dragoon guards, the other to the fourth dragoons; one is searching his pocket for money (not often to be found there) to purchase a drink of lemonade, from the Valentian seller of that refreshing beverage, who is handing a glass to a light dragoon. The heavies at that time (1811) wore plush breeches and a boot to the knee; the breeches never looked clean, and the boots were always dirty. The cocked hat, from being exposed to weather, and carelessly thrown down in camp, had acquired all sorts of curious shapes. At the latter end of George II.'s reign, as already mentioned, there were various kinds of cocks to the hats: the military cock and the mercantile, a hat cocked like a water-spout, another like a minced pie; and also the Kevenhuller. The old heavies perhaps had not one exactly like any of these; but it may safely be said, that every man had a cock of his own, regardless of any particular fashion. Some dragoons put scales to these hats, others leather straps or ribands, to secure them on the head, by tying them under the chin.

The figure on the left is a light dragoon, who has already received the Wellington trowser and boot, which were afterwards issued to all the cavalry.

Officers of the staff, and others who wore high cocked hats, soon found out the inconvenience of riding with a head-dress difficult to keep on. The commander-in-chief was the first to adopt a very low hat.

The officers of the army in the Peninsula ran into great extremes of fashion; and as there was a difficulty frequently in procuring articles of dress exactly according to regulation, considerable latitude was of necessity granted. An officer of the fourth dragoons who was very fond of being gaily dressed, was always in search of silver lace; and whenever he went into a town and returned to the camp, on being questioned regarding what articles of food were to be procured, his answer was, generally, "I don't know, but I found some silver lace."

Plate XXXIII. represents an officer on the staff, in 1811, one of heavy dragoons off duty, and an infantry officer. These are not exaggerated portraits. The hair was worn very long, and the waists longer, the sash being tied over the hips, the pantaloons tight about the waist, and very large at the lower part of the legs; the buttons on the waistcoat as few and far apart as possible; and those behind on the coat, also wide apart and very low down; the skirts of the coat very long. The hat on the figure on the right may be considered of the true Wellington pattern. The infantry officer at this period, wore a felt cap, a jacket and epaulette or epaulettes, according to his rank; a field officer wearing two. A lieutenant-colonel had a crown on the straps; a major a star; a captain one epaulette on the right shoulder; a subaltern one on the left: there was also a difference in the size of the bullion.

The fourth figure in the group is the portrait of an assistant-surgeon of the fourth dragoons, a despiser of dress, as may be perceived: he was

XXXIII.

A. D. 1811.

XXXIIII.

A.D 1812.

a clever man, and a close calculator of the rate of exchange upon England for the dollar, in which coin the army was paid (when it did get any pay). He went by the name of Six-and-eightpence, having cashed bills at this rate (being a saving man), the dollar being intrinsically worth only four and sixpence.

There was nothing in the jacket of the heavy and light dragoon at this period objectionable: the cocked hat was perhaps a bad head-dress for the heavy; and the helmet of the light dragoon, from being too high and over-weighted, was not a good one. The substitute of cloth trowsers and Wellington boots for plush and leather breeches and long boots was good; but there must have been some person in authority, or with influence in England, who had taken a great dislike to buttons, for in 1812 the heavy dragoon jacket was stripped of every button, and fastened in front with hooks and eyes; a wide piece of lace commencing at the top of the collar, running down the front, and turning to the right and left over the hips, terminated on small skirts, which opened as wide behind as before; much more ugly than the old jacket, without having any advantage. The helmet worn with this jacket was superior to the cocked hat. The light dragoons lost most of their buttons and their helmet; in exchange, they received a jacket with wide facings in front, and a felt shako. See Plate XXXIV.

The hussars, poor fellows! were taken no notice of, whether their dress was considered perfect, or whether any change was thought to be hopeless, it is difficult to ascertain; but while the heavy dragoons were relieved from *all* their buttons, and the light dragoons from *most* of theirs, the hussars were left covered with them, not only for use we may conclude, but for ornament; having five rows of buttons on the jacket they wore, put as close as they could be to each other, and five rows equally close on another jacket, which was carried loose slung round the neck, and falling over the left arm, called a pelisse.

The shako of the light dragoons was something similar to that used in the French army: the jacket was blue with wide facings, two small epaulettes, and a girdle round the waist.

The infantry was not much interfered with. It was imprudent at such a time, when actively employed in the field, to dress our light dragoons in the slightest degree like the troops of the enemy. The French army, from the revolution in 1789 to the period when the imperial forces were driven from Spain, was certainly not well dressed. Their infantry, after giving up the cocked hat, adopted the shako, a cap so heavy at the top, that many more of them were lost than of those of the British infantry in the field of battle. The dress of a portion of the French army is represented in Plate XXXV.

It is needless to point out the preposterous cap of the hussar, the short jacket, the wide trowsers, and two heavy belts over his shoulders, one for the pouch, the other to sling the carbine. The vain fashion of allowing the epaulettes dangling in front to display the rank of the wearer, is exemplified in the figure of the heavy dragoon, as well as in that of the gentleman with jockey boots, wearing a hat and feather of extreme height, who looks like any thing but a warrior.

The high hessian boots with large tassels suspended from the tops, the short skirts to the coat, and the shako of the light infantry man, are all in bad taste. Earrings in his ears complete his ridiculous appearance and unserviceable dress.

The heavy dragoon is the best appointed, though leather breeches and long boots are inconvenient on active service. The material of which the helmet was made was too thin for protection, and the crest too high for comfort.

It has already been mentioned, that the order of the Garter was founded in the twenty-second year of Edward III.'s reign: there were three orders added to it during this century:—

1st.—The order of St. Andrew, or the Thistle, the origin of which is very ancient, if we may believe John Guillim, who, in his "Display of Heraldry," writes:—"*Hungus* king of the *Picts*, the night before the battel was fought betwixt him and *Athelstan* king of *England*, saw in the skie a bright cross in fashion of that whereon *St. Andrew* suffered martyrdom; and the day proving successful to *Hungus*, in memorial of the said apparition which did presage so happy an omen, the *Picts* and *Scots* have ever since borne in their ensign and banner

XXXV.

A D. 1814

the figure of the said cross, which is in fashion of a saltier. And from hence it is believed that this order took its rise, which was about the year of our Lord, 810." It was revived by Queen Anne on the 31st Dec., 1703. The knights wear a green riband over the left shoulder, from which hangs the figure of St. Andrew, with his cross, in a circle of gold enamelled green, with the motto of the order, "Nemo me impune lacesset;" a collar composed of thistles and sprigs of rue linked together, enamelled green, with the figure of St. Andrew irradiated, pendant from it, encircled by the motto; and on the left breast a star, with four silver rays issuing between the points of the cross; upon a field crest, a thistle of gold and green encircled by the motto.

2nd.—The order of the Bath, which was instituted by Henry IV. in 1399, and revived by George I. in 1725.

3rd.—The order of St. Patrick, instituted by George III., Feb. 5, 1783.

On the change of the light dragoon's dress in 1812 to that represented in Plate XXXIV., the officers were also instructed to wear a jacket called a pelisse, as an undress. It was very plain, double-breasted, without ornament of any kind, with a rough shaggy lining; the cuffs and collar of the same, and of the colour of the facings of the regiment. Certainly it was not brilliant in appearance, and there was nothing about it to denote the officer; indeed it was not so gay as the clothing of the private dragoon; but it was very comfortable, put on and off in an instant; and on the dreadfully wet night preceding the battle of Waterloo, was found to be a most serviceable jacket.

At the close of the year 1815, it was thought prudent for the peace of Europe, to garrison an army of occupation in France: a large portion of the British army was ordered to remain, the other part returned to England. It was then determined by the authorities that four regiments of cavalry should be armed as lancers, and dressed like Poles; why they were to be so dressed merely because they were to carry lances is difficult to understand. The ninth, twelfth, sixteenth, and twenty-third light dragoons were the regiments selected for this arm; and Major Peters, a captain in the ninth light dragoons, was appointed to instruct detachments of these four regiments in the lance exercise, at the riding school at Pimlico. The dress selected for them was a jacket nearly of the same kind as that of the light dragoons, with the addition for the officers of an embroidered cuff and collar, a pair of enormous and expensively embroidered epaulettes, and an aiguillette. The cap was very high, with a square top, made of cane covered with cloth of the colour of the facings of the regiment, a brass plate in front, and a plume at the top of it; see Plate XXXVI. The private's dress corresponded, but brass scales were worn instead of epaulettes on the shoulders, with a cotton aiguillette. The Cossack trowser was worn by the officers, very full at the upper part, large indeed all the way down the legs, but diminishing gradually to the foot.

The infantry at this period wore a shako nearly similar to that of the French infantry: a short waist and short skirts to the coat; large trowsers were also the fashion of this arm of the service; officers on the staff wore a plain blue surtout coat, double breasted, the buttons in front being equidistant all the way down; the serviceable Wellington cocked hat was cast, and one of amazing height, much higher than that worn by George III. in Plate XXXI., was substituted, with a long feather for subordinate officers, and a large weeping plume for a general officer. This was copied from the Prussians.

There were several other changes during this reign. General officers at one time wore a cocked hat feathered round the edges.

XXXVI.

A. D. 1817

GEORGE IV.

A.D. 1820—1830.

It was said that George IV. was the most finished gentleman in Europe; this may have been so, but his good taste in dress was very questionable: he thought nothing becoming which did not fit tightly and smoothly on the person. The last portrait painted by Sir Thomas Lawrence of His Majesty sitting on a couch, is a convincing proof of this feeling. No doubt he is faithfully pourtrayed. His figure looks like a coat, breeches, and silk stockings tacked together, and then well stuffed with cotton. The soldier is certain to suffer from the bad taste of the sovereign in dress. George IV. said that in a military dress a wrinkle was unpardonable, but a seam was admissible. When the lancer dress for the officers was being selected, an officer of rank commanding one of the lancer regiments was ordered to attend George IV. (then Regent), to fit the new jacket on him; the tailor with a pair of scissors was ordered to cut smooth every wrinkle and finedraw the seams. The consequence was, that the coats of the private soldiers, as well as those of the officers, were made so tight they could hardly get into them; the freedom of action was so restricted, that the infantry with difficulty handled their muskets, and the cavalry could scarcely do the sword exercise.

At the coronation of George IV., on the 19th July, 1820, the household brigade, consisting of the two regiments of life guards, and the royal horse guards blue, appeared in bright cuirasses, which they continue to wear; they also had helmets of bright steel, with an enormous bearskin crest. This was the first time British troops had worn cuirasses since 1794, when they were given to some regiments of cavalry serving in the campaigns in Germany and the Netherlands; but finding them more cumbersome than convenient, they were deposited in store and never used again.

Plate XXXVII. represents a life-guardsman, a heavy dragoon, and a lancer of this period. The lancers had given up the aiguillette; the strongest advocate for finery could but acknowledge that a man's power was much crippled by the quantity of lines, straps, strings, and tassels he struggled under. The heavy cavalry had now a helmet so high that it "ignored" cut six of the sword exercise, and with the greatest difficulty could be kept on the head in a charge, or when the wind blew but moderately. Skirts were restored to the infantry jackets in this reign. The dress of the guards was somewhat altered. The sentry-boxes about the palace and public offices were increased in height to admit the sentries of the guards with an *improved* bearskin cap, the *improvement* being merely an addition to the height of it.

WILLIAM IV.

A.D. 1830—1837.

THERE were some few alterations in the dress of the army during this reign. Although William IV. had adopted the navy as his profession, towards the close of his reign he showed an inclination for military display, and paid great attention to the interior economy of the household troops. In 1834, the life guards and royal horse guards blue were given an enormous bearskin cap with a long feather on one side bending over the top; the weight and height of this cap rendered it so objectionable, that it was not long in use, and a steel helmet came again into wear. His Majesty inspected these regiments very closely not long before his death. The blues were paraded at the Regent's Park barracks, first mounted and then on foot, when a curious circumstance occurred. The king walked down the ranks asking many questions, and making many observations, and then placed himself at the usual spot to view the regiment as it marched past in parade order;

XXXVII.

A.D. 1824.

there were several noblemen and gentlemen close to His Majesty, amongst them Lord Skelmersdale, with whom he conversed: after the parade was over, and the king had departed, Lord Skelmersdale discovered that he had lost his watch. The circumstance was communicated to His Majesty, who, a few days afterwards, sent a handsome new watch to his lordship, requesting his acceptance of it, and pleasantly expressing his regret that he should have lost his own in such bad company.

William IV. was of opinion that all the army, except artillerymen and riflemen, should be dressed in the national colour—scarlet; consequently all the light cavalry, except the hussars, were changed, and regiments of the line were ordered to wear gold lace, and the militia silver; the facings of the navy at the same time were altered from white to scarlet. This was injudicious for outpost troops; and it was a subject of amazement to every body, that the uniform, in which our gallant navy had vanquished the enemy at St. Vincent's, the Nile, and at Trafalgar, and conquered in a hundred fights, should be superseded by one similar to the navies of most foreign powers.

QUEEN VICTORIA.

A.D. 1837—1852.

We have now arrived at the reign of our Most Gracious Majesty, Queen Victoria, a reign already longer than the last, and we may fondly hope that only a small portion of it has passed. Soon after Her Majesty ascended the throne the original dress was restored to the navy. The blue and white facings now again remind us of the noble deeds done in times past by those who wore them.

The light dragoons, also, recovered the colour of the dress they had so long served in; they were ordered to appear in blue, excepting one regiment of lancers. The sixteenth was selected to remain in scarlet; it may be considered a mark of distinction, and no regiment in the British cavalry is more deserving of favour from the sovereign. The regiment was raised in 1759, from which date it has been employed in active service out of England nearly forty years, in Portugal, in America, in Flanders, and throughout the Peninsular war; at the battle of Waterloo, at the siege and capture of Bhurtpore, in the invasion of Afghanistan, and lastly, in the bloody battles fought against the Sikhs on the banks of the Sutledj; with increasing honour and unvarying good conduct.

The dress of the Highland regiments has been but little, if ever altered. It is brilliant and picturesque in appearance, and perhaps national. The seventy-fourth regiment, now serving at the Cape of Good Hope, is entitled "Highlanders," but the men have not worn the bonnet or the kilt. Plate XXXVIII. represents a private of a Highland regiment in marching order, and a man of the seventy-fourth in fighting order. Had the men of this regiment been dressed in bonnets and kilts, as other Highland regiments, it would have been their duty to have followed the Caffres through the jungles and fastnesses of Southern Africa, with a towering plumed cap on their heads, and nothing to protect their nether parts from thorns and briers. The commander-in-chief at the Cape of Good Hope, from long experience inured to warfare, was perfectly aware, that, however imposing in appearance such a dress might be on a home parade ground, it is very ill adapted to Caffre warfare. The cap of the seventy-fourth, though not nearly so high as the Highland bonnet, was changed for a low one, and a dark blouse displaced the scarlet jacket; these, with some other alterations, fitted the soldier for the arduous war in which he is engaged, and rendered him a less conspicuous mark for the rifle of the enemy.

The household cavalry have again had their helmet altered; it is still steel with brass ornaments, but a weeping plume rises from the centre of the top and falls down on all sides. The dragoon guards and dragoons have a similar helmet, and they have had the skirts of

XXXVIII.

A.D. 1851.

XXXIX.

A.D. 1852.

XL.

A D 1852

their coats cut short, making their jacket nearly what it was when our army served in the Peninsula from 1808 to 1812.

The infantry have a new cap: one had been proposed formed something like a round hat with a rim; the present one, however, was selected in preference.

Plates XXXIX. and XL. represent different arms of the service in the dresses worn at this time—1852.

THE ARMIES OF INDIA.

EVERY Englishman must, more or less, feel an interest in the soldiers called Sepoys, who form the principal strength of the armies which hold our vast territories in India. When the first association of merchant adventurers, trading "*to the East Indies, and other islands and countries thereabouts*," obtained the royal assent and charter in the year 1600, and established the first factory in Surat in 1612, they were without soldiers. The Island of Bombay, ceded to Charles II. by the Portuguese in 1662, was afterwards transferred to the East India Company, and in 1687 was made the presidency of Western India, when it is probable there were a few soldiers there as a garrison. But Captain Arthur Broome, in his "History of the Bengal Army," writes, "the jealousy of the Mogul government was watchful in preventing the establishment of any military power in the country: the principal factory in Bengal in 1652 was at Hoogly, and constructed under the supervision of the officers of that government, who exercised the utmost vigilance to prevent the erection of any building which could possibly render the place convertible into a station of defence; the establishment of armed retainers was moreover strictly limited to *an ensign and thirty men to do honour to the principal agents*, which little band may be looked upon as the nucleus of the present extensive army maintained by the Company in the Bengal Presidency." Their soldiers were dressed in the native costume, with a colour, or a badge, to distinguish them as belonging to the Company.

In 1678, the military establishment was gradually increasing. In 1680, the English, for the first time in Bengal, were to be seen acting in open hostility to the native authorities. In 1683, the establishment was increased by two hundred and fifty European troops. The Company's native force was augmenting yearly, and the dress of the Sepoy gradually deviating from the oriental costume. The year 1757 found Colonel Clive, afterwards Lord Clive, in command of a considerable force, both Europeans and natives, whose gallantry gained the important victory of Plassey. At this period the native officers' dress was that represented in Plate XLI., in which there are two Sepoys, and a naik, or corporal, of another corps retaining the native costume and arms. It has been considered desirable to assimilate as much as possible the English and native soldiers in the Company's service: the Sepoys are well instructed in European tactics, and their dress is now nearly that of the royal army.

In 1826, at the siege of Bhurtpore, the Bengal Native Infantry were clad like the Sepoy pourtrayed in Plate XLII., in which there are also represented two of Skinner's Horse: the latter has always been a distinguished corps, and was very useful at that siege; the men wore a yellow tunic, with the upper part scarlet, ornamented with some curiously shaped pieces of black sheepskin. Their helmets were made of polished steel, of rather a conical shape, with a nasal, or guard for the nose, which slipped up and down at pleasure. This protection for the nose is common on Oriental head-pieces; it was used at a very early period in Europe: it is shown in the Norman dress in Plate III., as well as on the helmet, No. 11, in Plate XXV. This helmet of Skinner's Horsemen was well shaped to protect the head from the blow of a sabre; it had no superfluous top weight, fitted the head well, and was secured by scales tying under the chin. Their saddle was of native make, covered with a scarlet and yellow cloth. Their arms were the matchlock, or lance, and tulwa (native sword). The irregular cavalry has lately been greatly increased in Bengal; they retain the native costume, which is a long tunic, and is of a different colour in almost every regiment—the prevailing colours are red, green,

XLI.

A.D. 1757.

XLII.

A.D 1826.

orange, and yellow: they are armed with the matchlock, lance, sword, and some with pistols. These troops are raised and paid in a different way from the regular cavalry, and at less expense; many officers think them a better description of soldier.

Difficulties have arisen at times regarding the clothing of the Hindoo troops: they have been known to object to wear any part of dress supposed to be made of leather fabricated from the hide of the cow or calf. The saddle of the cavalry, made of pig-skin, has also created a feeling of disgust among the Mahomedans. The Hindoo has religious scruples regarding the use of leather made from the hide of the sacred cow. The Mahomedan considers himself defiled if touched by any portion of the unclean pig. These superstitious feelings seem to have subsided, or perhaps the men no longer care to inquire from what materials their equipments are made. It is, however, wrong and imprudent to insult their religious feelings in any way. With regard to the saddle, it would be desirable to give the men a rough cloth to place over it, for they absolutely cannot ride on one made of smooth leather. There is every good reason for instructing the Sepoys in European tactics, which are superior to any known in India, and without such instruction the European and native regiments could not manœuvre together; but it admits of a doubt if it has been wise to clothe the Sepoy so thoroughly in the European costume. There are many parts of the dress of the royal army exceedingly inconvenient to the English soldier, and ill adapted for their intended purpose. To a native of India, then, accustomed from infancy to a light and loose clothing, the tight European dress, when worn for the first time, must be disgusting; there are parts of it, indeed, to which he never becomes reconciled. It is to be concluded, that the object of dressing the European and native soldier alike is to deceive an enemy as to the strength of the English portion of the force: this, however, can scarcely happen, for when a British force takes the field in India, there are plenty of intelligent spies who immediately give every information regarding that force to the enemy. When the contending armies approach each other, a red jacket cannot disguise a black face.

At the disastrous period, after our army had been destroyed on the retreat from Cabool, and while Sale was gallantly defending Jellalabad, that distinguished soldier Nott was holding Candahar with but a small force, surrounded by a numerous enemy: he was short of ammunition, without a rupee in the treasury, and there was no medicine for the sick and wounded. General England having failed once in attempting to relieve him, marched a second time from Quettah on the 26th April, 1842: on the 30th, having entered the defile leading to the Kojuck Pass, "his force" (Kaye, in his "History of the War in Afghanistan," writes) "was locked up at the entrance to the Pass, whilst Wymer, with the Bengal regiments, was gallantly crowning the Kojuck, and reporting every thing clear for the advance of the Quettah brigade. The Sepoys of those three noble regiments, the 'Second,' 'Sixteenth,' and 'Thirty-eighth,' who would have followed Wymer wherever he pleased to lead them, were climbing the precipitous ascents, *disengaged of whatever might clog their movements.*" Colonel Stacey's narrative explains what did clog their movements; he writes, "these fine fellows had been led forward by Colonel Wymer at day-break, to occupy the heights commanding the Pass from Chummemo to the western side, to secure General England's party a safe passage. I have never seen our Sepoys to such advantage. *It was impossible to climb the precipitous hills in pantaloons; this part of their dress had therefore been discarded, and the men were in their doties:* as they showed on every accessible point they were the admiration of all."

Volumes might be written on these objectionable pantaloons without effect; but here is quoted the report of Colonel Stacey, an officer high in rank, and of great experience in the Company's service, who states that it was *impossible* for the Sepoys to climb the precipitous heights in pantaloons. Will the Sepoy continue to be *clogged* with this part of dress, apparently so ill suited to his habits, after such a record? To those who have never visited India a description of the dotie is, perhaps, desirable:—it is a long cloth passed round the waist, then falling down is carried round each thigh, reaching nearly to the knees, the end is brought up between the legs, and secured by tucking it in at the back

XLIII.

A.D. 1842.

of the waist. The legs are left bare from the knee to the shoe, the limbs free and unrestrained: most Sepoys wear the dotie under the pantaloons. When Wymer's men took off their pantaloons and retained the dotie, it may be compared to English workmen, who strip off their coats to work with greater freedom in their shirt sleeves. The Sepoys in Plate XLI. have rather a fanciful dotie, ornamented with a vandyke edging; it is shorter than that usually worn.

The shako has also been found to be inconveniently formed for service. When the "illustrious garrison of Jellalabad" crossed the river Sutlej near Ferozepore, on the 16th December, 1842, by two bridges of boats constructed for the purpose, the Sepoys of the thirty-fifth Bengal Native Infantry, distinguished by their gallant conduct as part of that garrison, were dressed as represented in Plate XLIII. The shako was not worn, a low cap covered with a white case was substituted: over the red jacket they had a well-tanned sheepskin, with the wool outwards, called in Afghanistan a Posteen; the Afghans use it as a warm dress during their severe winter. Some of these posteens are made long, falling below the knees.

One of the figures in Plate XLIII. is a private of the fifth Bengal Cavalry, two squadrons of which regiment formed part of the Jellalabad garrison, and were conspicuous for their gallant bearing throughout that trying service, under the command of that brilliant cavalry officer, the late Lieutenant-colonel Oldfield, then a captain. The other figures in the Plate are a private of irregular horse, and a Goorka, one of a small muscular brave race inhabiting the hills bounding our north-eastern frontier: they are dressed in dark green, and carry rifles. They partake of the character of the Chinese in their countenances.

When any new dress or equipment appears in the royal army, the Company's troops speedily adopt the same, without rejecting what may be unsuited to the climate of India, or considering what may be inconvenient to the Sepoy; and regardless of expense to the officers.

In the hot season, both the Royal and Company's troops wear white jackets and trousers, which are well calculated during excessive heat for the comfort of the men. This dress, when well made, is far from unbecoming. It might be supposed that on all parades, when the privates wear it, the officer would be instructed to appear in the same; but it is not so. The native soldiers of India, accustomed all their lives to the burning climate of that country, and who naturally suffer less from extreme heat, frequently appear on parade in a white jacket, while the European officers are buttoned up to the throat in one of scarlet cloth. At the mess-table, where a relaxation from the trammels of parade should be allowed, many commanding officers, more particularly of the royal army, insist on a cloth jacket being worn by the officers. When the thermometer is at 100°, which is frequently the case, and the atmosphere of the mess-room becomes more oppressive from the fumes of hot dishes, and the crowd of native servants in attendance, a white jacket is a cool and cleanly luxury. The cloth jacket, discoloured by profuse perspiration, is intolerable. Many officers are driven from the mess-table by this inconsiderate order. There are dinners given on particular occasions, when it is right that the officers should appear in full dress; but at the every-day mess they might be allowed to meet in good fellowship and kindly feeling their brother officers, to enjoy an agreeable and convivial meal, without the curse of wearing a coat distressing and disgusting.

XLIIII.

A.D. 1625-1824.

HATS AND HELMETS.   119

PLATE XLIV.

During the reign of Charles I., the Commonwealth, and the reigns of Charles II., James II., and William III., hats were worn with very wide rims, with feathers. The inconvenience of these rims being at length perceived, first one, and then two flaps were turned up, until about the time of Queen Anne, when the third flap was turned up, and the regular cocked hat formed. Various kinds were for the ensuing seventy or eighty years in vogue, as already mentioned in pp. 87, 98. In this Plate the following hats and helmets are pourtrayed:—

No. 1, a hat of the time of Charles I.

No. 2, a hat of the time of William III.

No. 3, the Nivernois hat.

No. 4, the Kevenhuller.

No. 5, the Ramilies.

No. 6, the Wellington.

No. 7, the hat worn by officers on the staff in 1830.

No. 8, the helmet of the 22nd light dragoons in 1760.

No. 9, the helmet of the 20th light dragoons in 1790.

No. 10, the helmet of all light dragoons in 1809.

No. 11, the heavy dragoon helmet in 1812.

No. 12, the heavy dragoon helmet in 1824.

REVIEW OF THE DRESS OF PAST TIMES.

HAVING described the dress of warriors from the earliest period of English history, during the time that armour was worn, as well as since it has been disused, it may be profitable to reflect on the numerous changes which have taken place, for the purpose of deciding if they have been progressive improvements, or the mere caprice of fancy and fashion.

When armour was in use, and men had to carry such a ponderous dress, it was a great object to unite lightness with strength, and give iron all the flexibility possible. Newly invented offensive weapons rendered it frequently necessary to alter defensive armour; but a variety of frivolous changes took place, and ornaments were added, evidently not necessary, on account of those weapons. The same desire for change and finery existed quite as much in those days as it does at present, and armour was decorated in the richest and most expensive style, and fashion was, as now, studied, regardless of utility. There are instances on record when the weight and heat of armour have caused the wearer to faint, and in some instances to be suffocated. It is said that some knights have gone to battle in armour so brilliant and of such great value, that when taken prisoners, they have been destroyed on account of it. We might be inclined to agree with King James I., who said, that "armour was an excellent invention; for it not only saved the life of the wearer, but prevented his killing any body else," did not history relate the fearful carnage which took place when it was worn.

The caprice of fashion is not peculiar to the present day; it was followed as devotedly, and with greater absurdity, in the olden time. Enormous sums of money were expended on suits of armour, and fashion was constantly varying some parts of them. At one time the cuirass was long, at another short-waisted; the breast of it assumed different shapes, from globose to angular; and the shape of the tapul was frequently changed. The toe of the solleret was at one time of enormous length, pointing down; at another time, equally long, pointing up; then the front of the solleret changed to square, and was sometimes six inches wide; and round toes were at one time in fashion. There were various other fashions; amongst them the curious ornaments which rose from the shoulders like wings, called ailettes, without any apparent use: they are shown on one of the figures in Plate IX.

The dress of private soldiers, probably, did not partake of the frivolities of fashion to such an extent; but no doubt they suffered from it. Knights, armed for the jousts, were not clad as they went to war. At the jousts, being immediately under the bright eyes of their lady-loves, they profusely bestowed the greatest splendour on themselves and on their horses. Magnificent plumes waved from the crests of their helmets, as well as from their horses' heads. They were both emblazoned with heraldry, and enriched with gold and silver; the horses, loaded and covered with rich trappings, staggered under the great weight they had to carry. The beautiful proportions of the human figure seem ever to be disregarded, and never taken as a guide for the clothing put upon it. The body is to be warped and distorted into any shape that fashion may dictate.

During several reigns, civilians ran into such extremes of fashion, that sumptuary laws were enacted to check those absurdities; but they were evidently framed with the view of supporting the distinctions of rank.

Nothing can be more ridiculous than the figure called an antick, in Plate XXIV.; yet there are instances, at an earlier period than when this antick flourished, when tomfoolery was practised to excess. At one time, dandies had the toes of their shoes so long, that they could not have walked had they not been suspended from their knees, which they were by light chains.

Such absurdities, however, could not extend to the military; and it may be observed, that warriors did not hamper themselves with much unnecessary clothing when they took the field.

In Plate IV., there are Assyrian helmets of as early a date as 800 years before Christ: they are taken from drawings in "Layard's Nineveh." It is evident that No. 2 was the fighting man's helmet; and Nos. 1 and 3 were worn at the pomp and parade of war. The Greek helmets, Nos. 4 and 5, in the same Plate, savour much of the same character as the latter. No. 8 looks like a head-dress to do good work in; and it was in such helmets that the Romans conquered the world.

Amongst forty-one drawings of helmets in the preceding Plates, which were used in former days, there are only seven from the top of which excrescences rise; the others are warlike looking.

In the strife between the houses of York and Lancaster, when this land was overrun with war, there are scarcely any soldiers described as wearing high helmets. That numbered 14, in Plate XV., was found in Bosworth Field.

There was, perhaps, no period when soldiers were better clad for battle, or when they needed it more, than in Cromwell's days, though the boots of the cavalry may, from the size of the tops, have been rather inconvenient. His soldiers have been called stern plebeian sectarians; and we are told that they were originally composed of tapsters' decayed serving men, mechanics, and such like; nevertheless, they were Englishmen, and being well-dressed, armed, and disciplined for war, made excellent soldiers, before whom the high-spirited chivalry of England went down.

All the helmets, morions, and pots in Plate XXV. are without any tall ornament at the top of them; they are close-fitting, warlike head-dresses, sufficiently raised from the head to prevent concussion from a blow, and strong enough to protect it from the cut of a sabre. Most of them have scales to guard the cheek and secure the helmet on the head by tying under the chin. Behind they have overlapping plates of thin iron, sewn on leather, to protect the back of the neck. No. 11

has a nasal, or guard for the nose, which is moved up and down at pleasure.

The tunic is certainly one of the most ancient garments known. It may be seen in the sculptures and paintings of early Egypt. It was in constant use by the Greeks, and ultimately adopted by the Romans. It has been worn in England in a variety of forms and lengths until the end of the fifteenth century. The word was applied to the military surcoat: indeed it appears in all ages to have been the prevailing garment. The present convenient and comfortable coat, called surtout, which does not appear likely to go out of fashion, is nothing but a modified tunic.

It may be said, that the uniform of the British army dates from the commencement of the eighteenth century. Scarlet and blue had long been the two principal colours of the cloth ordered for the array of the king's troops, in accordance with the blazon of the royal standard; the guide from the commencement of heraldry, for the liveries of retainers, having been the armorial bearings of their lord or leader.

But the men-at-arms were, during the early periods of our history, covered with mail or plate; and of the lighter armed troops, the smallest number perchance was brought into the field by the sovereign himself, the host, comprising the contingents of the barons, and the followers of every knight in it, wore the colours of the particular banners they served and fought under. A white cross was the general badge of the English troops in the time of the Crusades, and was worn as late as the reign of Edward IV.

In Henry VIII.'s time we find soldiers in white coats with a red cross. Stow speaks of the marching watch wherein the archers wore coats of white fustian, signed on the breast and back with the arms of the city of London (at that time a red cross).

In the sixteenth and seventeenth centuries scarfs of the royal colours, or family badges, were worn by officers, either over the shoulder or round the waist, and sometimes round the arm.

As armour became abandoned, the necessity for uniform became more apparent, and scarlet with blue facings was definitively established as that of the British army during the reign of Queen Anne, at which time the pike ceased to be carried, and the musket and socket-bayonet became the general weapons of the infantry. The cartridge-box supplied the place of the bandolier, every species of body armour was discarded, the gorget, which had been a protection to the breast, dwindling into the ornamental trifle now known by that name. The red and white feather was worn in this reign. The black cockade appeared about the time of George II.: it was assumed by the house of Hanover in opposition to the white cockade, the well-known badge of the Jacobite party.

An extract from a work of much merit by Field-Marshal Saxe, entitled "Reveries; or, Memoirs upon the Art of War," published in 1762, and translated from the French, may be well introduced here. He writes—"Our dress is not only expensive but inconvenient, no part of it being made to answer the end required; the love of appearance prevails over the regard due to health, which is one of the grand points demanding our attention. I would have a soldier wear his hair short, and be furnished with a small wig, grey or black, made of lamb-skin, which should be put on in bad weather; this wig will resemble the natural head so well as to render it almost impossible to distinguish the difference; will fit well when properly made, costs but twenty-pence, and lasts during life; it will be very warm, prevent colds and fluxes, and give quite a good air. Instead of a hat I would recommend a helmet made after the Roman model, which will be no heavier, be far from inconvenient, protect the head against the stroke of a sabre, and appear extremely ornamental. I am at a loss to know why armour has been laid aside, for nothing is either so useful or ornamental: perhaps it may be said that the invention of gunpowder abolished the use of it, but that is far from being the true reason, because it was the fashion in Henry IV.'s (of France) reign, and since, to the year 1667, and every one knows that powder was introduced long before that time. All nations are reluctant, whether it proceeds from self-love, laziness, or folly, to relinquish old customs; even good institutions make their progress but slowly amongst us; for we are grown incorrigible in our prejudices, that such, whose utility is confirmed by the whole world, are notwithstanding frequently rejected by us; and then, to vindicate our exceptions upon every such occasion, we only say "'tis contrary to custom.'" He continues, "Nothing but indolence and effeminacy could have occasioned armour to be laid aside: to carry a cuirass or trail a pike during years, for the uncertain service of a single day, was deemed perhaps a hardship; but when a state so far degenerates as to suffer the discipline of its troops to be neglected, or convenience to supply the place of use, one may venture to foretell, without gift of prophecy, that its ruin is approaching. The Romans conquered the universe by the force of their discipline; and in proportion as it declined their power decreased. When the Emperor Gratian had suffered the legions to quit their cuirasses and helmets, because the soldiers, enervated by idleness, complained that they were too heavy, their success forsook them, and those very barbarians whom they had formerly defeated in such numbers, and who had worn their chains so many ages, became then their conquerors."

Writing of cavalry, he recommends "a rifled carbine which is loaded at the breech, by opening; thus speed in loading is increased, and a greater range obtained: the carbine to be slung over the shoulder, a pouch fixed to the waist-belt. The blades of the swords to be three-square, so as effectually to prevent an attempt to cut with them, which method of using a sword seldom does much execution, and to be four feet in length. Pistols to be totally laid aside; for they are only a superfluous addition of weight and incumbrance: the front rank to have lances, which Montecuculli, in his 'Memoirs,' prefers to all other weapons for cavalry, and says they are irresistible. The lance to be twelve feet long, the staff hollow, to weigh about six pounds. With regard to the bridle, I am far from approving of that with a bit; instead of which I would recommend a head-stall having two straight branches, and from the part where the bit is usually placed a leathern strap should pass over the horse's nose, this being contrived to draw close in proportion as the rider tightens his reins, will govern a horse effectually, and answer much better than any bit; one may stop and manage the most headstrong at pleasure, without spoiling his mouth or inflaming his jaws. There is considerable advantage attending this sort of bridle, in that a horse will be able to feed with it on as well as off; by only slackening the reins he is at full liberty to open his mouth, and by tightening them again he is compelled to shut it, which will prevent his lolling out his tongue, and put a stop to several bad customs which are learnt by the bit; it will moreover make him raise and carry his head well: it is, originally, the invention of Charles XII. of Sweden. With regard to the saddle, it is extremely defective; if a horse grows lean the bow bears on the shoulders and galls him; if he rolls on the ground he breaks it: besides, the buckles and other appurtenances are hurtful, expensive, and heavy. I have invented another: the bow is made of iron, strong and well tempered, and fixed on a pair of cloth or leathern pannels, stuffed with either wool or hair, to the end of which must be fastened the crupper, over this must be a black sheep-skin, or a skin of any animal, this skin to be brought across the horse's chest, underneath must go a circingle; the stirrup-leathers to be fastened at the bow of the saddle: these pannels and skins are never to be taken off the horses' backs, either by day or night, except to dress them. This entire equipage does not cost a third part so much as ours, is infinitely more convenient, weighs nothing, and never galls a horse's back. Every man to be furnished with a large sack seven feet in circumference and five feet deep, with slings to put the arm through; being filled with forage they are to be placed en croupe."

Plate XLV. represents a dragoon appointed, as Marshal Saxe proposes, in very light armour, with the noseband to the horse, and a sack of forage en croupe. A is the proposed saddle.

These "Memoirs" coming from so celebrated a warrior as Marshal Saxe, are worthy of consideration; his first remark, stating "our dress is not only expensive but inconvenient, no part of it being made to answer the end required; the love of appearance prevails over the regard due to health, which is one of the grand points demanding attention," is most applicable to the dress of the British army at this

XLV.

A

A.D 1762.

moment. His proposed grey or black lambskin cap might be very useful on active service. The superiority of the helmet over a hat is generally acknowledged. With regard to a continuation of armour, the Marshal's observation alludes to cavalry only, and it is difficult to believe that a horseman without armour can contend hand to hand on equal terms with a swordsman protected by a cuirass; yet the increased weight for the horse to carry, and in hot weather the suffocating heat of a cuirass to the wearer, renders it objectionable, and the answer of the life-guardsman, who distinguished himself by his prowess at Waterloo, is not to be disregarded, when asked if again engaged what dress he would prefer, said, "he should like to take off his coat and turn his shirt sleeves up over his elbows:" an answer showing how necessary this practical soldier thought the perfect freedom of the arm.

Marshal Saxe's assertion, that all nations are reluctant to relinquish old customs, is applicable to all people and to all times, as much so to the present as any other. Nobody will deny the justness of his remark when he writes, "when a state so far degenerates as to suffer the discipline of its troops to be neglected, or *convenience to supply the place of use*, one may venture to foretell, without gift of prophecy, that its ruin is approaching." God forbid that this should be applicable to our country; yet moving our troops by railways instead of marching them from one quarter to another, allowing them to retain inferior arms, and limiting the use of ammunition for ball firing to so small a quantity that the soldier cannot possibly acquire the perfect use of his weapon, is very like neglecting the discipline of troops, and allowing convenience to supply the place of use. It is very doubtful if a rifle carbine is a good weapon for a mounted man, even if loading at the breach should be perfectly successful, because the unsteadiness of the horse would destroy accuracy of firing. With regard to loading at the breach, General Sir Howard Douglas, in his treatise on small arms, (which all military men should read), writes, "the breach loading muskets for general service appear to be failures, and will no doubt be condemned as arms for general service, however useful they may be in the hands of a few expert men for special purposes;" notwithstanding this remark, there can be no doubt, provided the loading at the breach could be made perfect, rapidity of firing would be greatly increased. Marshal Saxe says, "the blades of the swords to be three-square, so as effectually to prevent an attempt to cut with them, which method of using a sword seldom does much execution, and to be four feet in length."

Napoleon was evidently of opinion that the point of the sword was more destructive than the edge. At the battle of Wagram his anxiety was extreme as the cuirassiers of the guard passed him at a quick trot. He is described by Alison, in his "History of Europe," as "plunging his sword in the air;" he exclaimed, "No sabreing; give point! give point!"

There is no doubt that more mortal wounds are made by the point than by the edge of the sabre. If the point alone is to be used, it is, as Marshal Saxe observes, desirable to make the swords three square, effectually to prevent an attempt to cut with them. Four feet, though a great length, is perhaps not too long for such a sword. It is desirable that troops so armed should be taught every description of point, and every guard against cuts, as well as to parry the point of an adversary, but prohibited from ever practising cuts; then they would not be likely to make mistakes. Cutting is more natural than making a point, and when a man has been taught both to cut and give point with a sword that is made for both purposes, he is certain to use the edge in preference to the point.

It is an error to make a sword cut and thrust; a well-shaped sabre for cutting cannot have a good point; and if the point is a good one, the properties of the sabre are destroyed. It may be doubtful whether the long sword, of which the point only can be used, or the sabre, is most useful in battle; for though the point is more deadly, the edge renders more men *hors de combat*. As an example, on the 11th of April, 1812, a very brilliant affair took place between our cavalry and that of the French near Llerena, in Estremadura. There were about 1900 swords drawn on each side. The French force consisted of the seventeenth dragoons, the twenty-seventh dragoons, the twenty-first chasseurs, and the second hussars; the British regiments were the fifth dragoon guards, the third and fourth dragoons, and the twelfth and sixteenth light dragoons. It was not a long affair; the enemy stood our charge, and then gave way. They had about twelve men killed, and lost one hundred and twenty-eight prisoners, nearly all of whom were wounded by cuts. We had nine men killed and forty-seven wounded. It appeared that all the former were killed by the point, and most of the latter wounded by the edge. One hundred and twenty-eight prisoners would not have been made had not the majority of them been wounded; showing, that the wounds from the point, in this affair, were mostly mortal, but the edge of the sabre rendered more *hors de combat*.

Marshal Saxe writes, "pistols to be laid aside, for they are only a superfluous weight and incumbrance." Certainly there are but few cavalry officers, who served during the Peninsular war, that ever saw a pistol used, unless to light a fire in bivouac, and to shoot a glandered or wounded horse.

Unfortunately, it is not so in India; the native cavalry had a practice, when ordered to charge, of drawing their pistols instead of their swords. It is to be hoped that this erroneous method is left off.

Marshal Saxe recommends the front rank to have lances twelve feet long, the staff hollow, to weigh about six pounds. There are few experienced military men who doubt the power of the lance. The front rank using the lance, and the rear rank supporting with the sword, (the lance being slung on the bridle arm,) is a most formidable array, and probably much more so than both ranks using the lance. The point of the lance cannot be too sharp or too finely tapered; but it is not an outpost weapon. The most powerful cavalry should be armed with the lance, outpost troops with the carbine.

Marshal Saxe's suggestion to use a running strap over the nose of the horse, instead of a bit, may be a very good one; for in the field it would be an amazing advantage to have the horses always ready to mount; the delay in bridling is the greatest that occurs. A squadron of the thirteenth light dragoons, forming part of General Beresford's army, which had been pushed across the Guadiana at Juramanha, on the 7th of April, 1811, preparatory to the first siege of Badajos, was surprised by a considerable force, sent by the French General, Latour Manbourg, to discover if the British army was about to cross the river. A major, a lieutenant, and between fifty and sixty men and horses of the 13th dragoons, were made prisoners. One officer made his escape by jumping on his horse without a bridle, and, turning his head in the direction of the British camp, let him go his best pace, and escaped. It was thought at the time that others might have escaped had the horses been bridled. If the horse is effectually governed, as Marshal Saxe asserts, by the nose-band, the plan is worth a trial; yet as no troops have adopted it, probably it does not answer.

The saddle recommended by Marshal Saxe, as superior to the one then in use, no doubt was so. The saddles used at the commencement of the Peninsular war by our cavalry were, both for heavy and light, made on the same principle; the defects of them were exactly what this old warrior mentions: "If a horse grows thin, the bow bears on the shoulders and galls him; if he rolls on the ground, he breaks the saddle." Many were the dreadfully galled withers of our horses before it was found necessary, when the horses became thin, to roll a blanket in a certain way, and place it under the saddle, which kept it clear of the back-bone and withers.

The hussar saddles now used by our light cavalry can never wring the withers; but they are very liable to be broken by the horses rolling.

The sack mentioned by Marshal Saxe, for forage, does not seem to be so well adapted to the purpose as the nets which our cavalry used in Spain.

The curious volume by Stewart, the Hair-dresser, published in 1782 under the astounding name of "*Plocacosmos;* or, the whole Art of Hair-dressing," furnishes us with many full-blown examples of the monstrous, which then passed for the height of taste. Two are copied in Plate XLVI. At no period in the history of the world was any thing more absurd in head-dress than the one here depicted (see No. 1). The body of this erection was formed of tow, over which the hair was turned, and false hair added in great curls, bobs, and ties, pomatumed and pow-

XLVI.

A.D. 1782-1831.

dered to profusion; then hung all over with very large rows of pearls, or glass beads—fit only to decorate a chandelier; flowers as obtrusive were stuck about this heap of finery, which was surmounted by broad silken bands, and ostrich feathers, until the head-dress of a lady added three feet to her stature; and the male sex, to use the words of the "Spectator," became suddenly dwarfed beside her.

To effect this, much time and trouble was wasted, and great personal annoyance was suffered. Heads, when properly dressed, "kept for three weeks," as the barbers phrased it; that they would not "keep" longer, may be seen by the many recipes they give for the destruction of insects which bred in the powder and pomatum. The description of opening a lady's head, after a three weeks' dressing, given in the magazines of this period, it would be imagined, would have taught the ladies common sense; but fashion could stifle even the disgust that must have been felt by all.

The second drawing, No. 2, of a lady's head-dress, is another specimen of taste. The lady in the original print (one of Carrington Bowles'), is intended to represent the fair Mary Anne Robinson, the first love of the prince, afterwards King George IV. It can scarcely be imagined, that a really lovely woman could so disfigure herself; yet any idea of absurdity in this fashion was never entertained by any body at that period. The lady is termed the "Bird of Paradise" in the original engraving, and the whole thing is meant as seriously as a sermon.

Now, opposite to the first lady's head-dress, of 1782, is drawn the cap of the foot guards in the year 1851; and opposite to the "Bird of Paradise," that of the horse artillery in the same year. It may be difficult to decide, whether the ladies' or the military head-dresses here pourtrayed are the most preposterous. The latter certainly have the advantage in one respect; they can be taken off when the soldiers go to bed. If, however, ladies went to battle, theirs would then decidedly have the advantage, because the protection to the head would be better, and no military weapon could remove them from their places.

With regard to dress, the term beautiful is certainly conventional. Surely the lady's head, No. 1, is more beautiful, or, to speak more truthfully, not so ugly as the grenadier cap opposed to it; and the great cap of the horse artilleryman can bear no comparison, as to beauty, with the head of the "Bird of Paradise."

There is no exaggeration in these drawings. Few of us are aware how quickly good taste becomes vitiated by preposterous fashions. The eye long accustomed to a certain costume is offended at first by any change, nevertheless it soon becomes reconciled, and then, however ridiculous the dress may be, it is deemed "the thing:" otherwise, how is it possible such a head-dress as No. 1 could ever have been worn? How could that of the "Bird of Paradise" for a moment have been tolerated? How could such a cap as the grenadier's ever have been adopted? and how could any person in authority have ordered such a cap as that opposite the "Bird of Paradise" to be placed on the head of a soldier? The bear-skin of which these caps are made is not a bad material; it is not much affected by heat, cold, or rain, and is difficult to cut through with a sabre; and if the top weight was considerably reduced by diminishing the height and wearing it without a feather, it might be a serviceable cap, and be made much handsomer by introducing the royal arms or some other device on the front. Let any one compare the foot-guardsmen walking through the streets of London on a week-day in their forage-caps, with the same men on Sunday staggering along under an enormous bear-skin cap nearly eighteen inches high. In the first case they appear to be fine athletic active fellows, moving with a free and graceful step, and with the power of turning their heads to the right or left, up or down, at pleasure. In the second case, they move under a ponderous head-dress, which, from its disproportioned size, makes the men absolutely look diminutive; their action is constrained, they dare not look up or down, scarcely to the right or left, and they appear to be balancing the cap on their heads, as a juggler poises a sword on his chin; they are obliged to regulate the motions of the body in such a manner as not to disturb the equilibrium of their head-dress. Is this a fit cap for a warrior? When reviews take place in Hyde Park before persons of high rank, colonels of regiments (though general officers) frequently march past at the head of their regiments.

To see the Duke of Wellington march by in a grenadier cap, similar to that just described, is a painful sight to those who served under him in the Peninsular war, and recollect the plain surtout and the snug cocked hat this great man used to wear, so well calculated for activity, and the rapid movements his wonderful mind might desire to carry into practice.

There are persons who imagine that dress is not necessary any further than to cover our nakedness; and there are others inclined to devote too much attention to it; yet there are none, having a particular pursuit to follow, who will not adopt, as far as is in their power, a dress made for the purpose. Do not those who play at cricket, rackets, tennis, or any other violent game, wear dresses admitting of perfect freedom, and made of materials calculated to prevent sudden chills, after profuse perspiration? Who on going to a tropical climate does not prepare dresses for excessive heat? and who visiting extreme cold does not provide warm clothing? Again, let it be asked, What sportsman when he shoots is not equipped as he thinks best adapted to that pursuit? or who amongst huntsmen neglect to dress themselves appropriately? It is true that few sportsmen take the field in the same dress, nor do they carry their ammunition in the same manner, but all agree that a hat or cap should neither be high in the crown, nor heavy, and that it should be firm on the head, so as not to fall off when the wearer jumps a ditch, or runs. All agree that shoes should not pinch, or make the feet sore: and when shooting in woods it is agreeable to be protected from thorns and briers: and all also agree that if their limbs are in any way confined by a tight dress, they cannot go through a long day's shooting.

Fox-hunters may vary the cut and colour of their coats according to fancy, and differ regarding the materials of which their breeches and waistcoats should be made; but the old sportsman, grown wise from experience, knows that a high-crowned hat resists the air too much for speed, that it is exceedingly inconvenient when brushing through woods, or bull-finching (as it is termed) over thick hedges; moreover, that it is no protection to the head in a fall. He therefore wears the close-fitting hunting cap, so perfectly adapted to the purpose for which it was invented, and which has saved many men's lives. He removes two useless buttons which tailors always put in the skirts of the coat, because he knows he may be wounded by them in the part he sits down upon: and the buttons at the knees he discards, having suffered when there has been a large field of sportsmen crowding through a gateway by having those buttons pressed into his flesh. These are points carefully looked to by individuals; surely it is but due to our soldiers, who cannot be allowed to use their own discretion in these matters, that the clothing, arms, and appointments provided for them, should be of good materials, and perfectly adapted to the purposes of war. Would any person adopt our foot soldier's dress and musket to go out shooting? Could any fox-hunter be found who would hunt in a head-dress like that worn by our cavalry, either heavy or light dragoon, lancer or hussar? No sensible man would do the one or the other. The infantry musket would knock any body up before he had half finished his day's sport; the tight jacket would restrict his movements; the cap would be lost in the first ditch he jumped over; and he would with difficulty load his gun from the pouch in which ammunition is carried. The cavalry helmet or cap would not remain on the fox-hunter's head for five minutes.

These may be considered by some overstrained comparisons, yet the foot soldier requires a dress in which he has the unrestricted use of his limbs, a cap that will not fall off when he runs, one that will protect his eyes from the glare of the sun, and his head from the blow of a sabre: he requires shoes of such a description in which he can perform long marches without blistering his feet. The musket and bayonet are his only weapons of attack and defence, they should therefore be very well made, and of the lightest kind consistent with safety. The infantry soldier in 1851 carried, in heavy marching order, without his musket, bayonet, and sling, and without ammunition, thirty-nine pounds, thirteen ounces; his musket, bayonet and sling weighs eleven pounds fourteen ounces, sixty rounds of ammunition, with seventy-five copper caps, weighs about five pounds five ounces, making fifty-seven pounds; add to this three days' provision and a blanket, amounting at least to eleven pounds, which on service he would frequently have to carry, makes the whole weight sixty-eight pounds; under this weight he may march from ten to fifteen miles a day for a succession of days: he may have to move in front of the enemy all day, sometimes running, sometimes fighting; it may be through rough and muddy roads, in rain, or cold, or heat, still the foot soldier must move and carry this load, enduring hunger, thirst, and fatigue.

The duties of the cavalry soldier in the field are occasionally more like the work of the fox-hunter than is generally supposed, though in England it is desirable to give the cavalry horses no more work than will keep them in good condition, ready to meet any emergency, and to preserve them as long as possible efficient in the service; yet during the Peninsular war the cavalry at times had hard and fatiguing duties, and rapid work to perform. In the retreat to Corunna, and in the retreat from Burgos, there were frequent and speedy bursts. An affair which was not very unlike a fox-chase took place in Spain on the 16th April, 1811. The heavy brigade, commanded by the Honourable General De Grey, consisting of the third dragoon guards, and fourth dragoons, with the thirteenth light dragoons attached, marched on Los Santos, a town in Estremadura; about two miles short of it, the brigade was dismounted and the horses unbridled to feed; a patrole had been sent on to ascertain where the enemy was, which returned in great haste to report that Los Santos was full of French cavalry. The brigade bridled up as quick as possible, mounted and moved rapidly towards the place; on approaching which the French troops were seen turning out and forming on their parade ground; at first, only perceiving the thirteenth light dragoons, the enemy, consisting of the second and tenth hussars, were preparing to charge, but the heavy brigade coming in view, they turned and fled as fast as their horses could go: the thirteenth light dragoons pursued along the high road, the heavy brigade took a straighter line across the country, and going at their best pace, hoped to cut in on the enemy; the ground over which they went was intersected with several ditches, walls, and other obstacles, which shook a good deal the regularity of the pursuit. It was, however, maintained with great spirit for about eight miles, when all the horses being blown and many completely knocked up, the halt was sounded. Having made about one hundred and sixty prisoners, including two officers, the brigade returned to Los Santos. The pace had been too fast for the horses; there were few inclined to eat their corn that night, and twelve died from distress.

FIRE-ARMS.

THE most important part of a soldier's equipment is his arms. We seem to forget that the British infantry are armed with the musket and bayonet. It is an acknowledged fact, that precision of calculation and rapid movements are most essential in war, but rapid movements derive their importance not from the mere circumstance of placing columns of men in certain commanding positions, but from the deadly weapons with which they may be armed, and a thorough knowledge in the use of them. It would create no alarm in an army to be out-marched by an enemy, a mere host of unarmed men. A general would feel no anxiety at having the flank of his army turned by a force however superior, if he was convinced that force did not know how to use their arms. It is the deadly fire of the musket which renders infantry formidable; and if they are not taught the use of it, the bayonet of itself cannot prevent their destruction by a well instructed enemy. It would be better to return to the bow and arrows and the pike, than to arm our men with the musket and not teach them how to fire ball. The chief end of the soldier is to destroy the enemy by firing ball. The use of the manual and the drill is to give readiness and facility in handling the musket that is to fire ball. The use of all the field manœuvres, in which he has been trained, is to gain position and formation for the better firing of ball.

During the time of our Edwards and Henrys, our archers were renowned for the accuracy and rapidity of their flights of arrows; they were famed throughout Europe as the most formidable soldiers; they were the *élite* of our armies. But of what use could they have been, if, like our blank cartridge firing, they had been taught only to twang the bow instead of delivering the arrow?

It is a wonderful fact, that, during the war of a quarter of a century, the militia and volunteer force of the United Kingdom amounted nearly to half a million of men: they were almost all uninstructed in firing ball! Most fortunate was it for this country that Buonaparte had sufficient employment for his troops on the Continent, and did not land on our coasts 300,000 soldiers well disciplined and trained to ball firing.

Much was written some time since on the bayonet; it was called a crooked, ricketty zigzag, that seldom hit the mark when used offensively. Napoleon Buonaparte, a tolerable judge in these matters, pronounced, that when fitted on the musket, it was the most perfect combination of fire-arm and steel that ever was put into the hand of man. As a defensive weapon, the bayonet is effective against cavalry; while the sword in the hands of footmen could not defend them for a moment against the charge of horsemen. A square of infantry, with a hedge of bayonets bristling from the barrels of loaded muskets, the front rank kneeling, the men firm and resolute, may defy the attack of cavalry. The Russian general Suwarrow derided the bullet as an arrant fool, a wanderer on the wind, while he put the greatest confidence in the bayonet.

The distinction between the semi-barbarous and civilized soldier is here made. All savage tribes, not well instructed in fire-arms, are anxious to be led to the charge to decide at once by bodily strength the fate of the day. The civilized soldier, trained in due self-command, disappoints the fury of the savage by skilful manœuvre, and, in full confidence of the fire-arm in which he has been well trained, destroys the adversary before his weapon can be brought into use.

Modern warfare is misile warfare. It will scarcely be any thing else with infantry. The bullet will always prevail over the point; and a more perfect modern warrior cannot be exhibited, than a foot soldier well dressed and armed, obedient to command, self-possessed amidst the havoc and confusion of battle, with full confidence in his weapons, directing the fire of his musket, accurately and rapidly, with deadly effect. It is as unlike ancient warfare, with all the demoniac passions excited by a hand-to-hand combat, as possibly can be. Quickly and resolutely the well-trained soldier uses his weapon; and the best trained troops, led by brave and experienced officers, though the men may be inferior to the enemy in individual bodily strength, will feel confident of victory.

Of all weapons ever invented, the rifle is the most deadly. Our armies experienced the effect of it in America. The barbarous Caffres are now making us suffer from it at the Cape of Good Hope. At the battle of Jacinta (*vide* Kennedy's "Texas"), which sealed the fate of the Mexican army at Texas, a regular force of more than 1500 men, commanded by the experienced general Santa Anna, was destroyed in less than half an hour by a band of colonial riflemen, not amounting to half their number; but so deadly was their fire, that 630 of his force were killed outright, and 208 wounded, the comparatively small number of the latter proving the terrible accuracy of rifle practice. The rest of the Mexican army, appalled at this fearful execution, surrendered at discretion: and all this was achieved by the Anglo Americans at the small sacrifice of two killed and twenty-three wounded! Our New Orleans fight was a bad business, and Bunker's Hill was something akin to it; and the same thing must occur again and again, as long as troops, with indifferent arms, uninstructed in the use of them, and restrained by tight and inconvenient dress and equipment, are opposed to a vigilant enemy, who are perfect masters of well-constructed and deadly weapons.

It is astonishing, after so much experience, why we should be so reluctant to increase the rifle force of our army. There is a general feeling that the present dress of our troops requires change. Change, however, is of little use without improvement. All dress and equipment of the soldier should be subservient to the arms he carries, and the character of the service on which he is employed; but if his arms are bad, and he is not taught how to use them, it matters little in what dress he is to be slaughtered.

The continental powers spare no expense in arming and equipping their troops with all the best inventions of skill and science; we are content to allow our soldiers to carry a musket so heavy that it knocks them up on a march, and from its violent recoil makes them nervous to fire.

Kaye, in his well-written history of the Affghan war, describing Pollock's attack on the advance to Cabul, at Tazeen, writes, in page 579, " Gallantly the infantry ascended the heights on either side of the pass, and gallantly the Affghans advanced to meet them. The stormers of the thirteenth light infantry clomb the hills on the right, the ninth and thirty-first on the left; and as they went, hotly and thickly upon them poured iron rain from the Affghan jezails; but never for a moment, beneath the terrible fire that greeted them as they pushed up the hill side, did these intrepid soldiers waver. *They knew that their muskets were no match for the Affghan jezail. The enemy, indeed, seemed to deride them;* so having reached the hill top, they fixed their bayonets, and charged with a loud hurrah. The cold steel took no denial. Down went Affghan marksmen before the English bayonets; the foremost men stood to be pierced, and the rest, awed by the fall of their comrades, and the desperate resolution of the British troops, fled down the hill in confusion."

The inferiority of our musket is here made apparent; yet we are not to suppose that an unwieldy weapon like a jezail, which can scarcely be fired without a rest, and is loaded very slowly, although its range is great, would be a desirable substitute for our musket. But these jezails would have had no chance against experienced riflemen; and while our troops were storming the heights, the summits would have been cleared of the enemy by a well-directed fire from rifles.

From the following statement of the allowance of ball cartridge which is granted to our troops for practice, we can form a pretty good judgment of the prospect they have of becoming good marksmen. For each man of infantry regiments twenty rounds of ball and forty rounds of blank cartridges are issued in the spring, ten rounds of ball and twenty rounds of blank cartridges in the autumn; making a total of thirty ball cartridges and sixty blank for the practice of twelve months. Light infantry regiments are allowed ten rounds of ball cartridges more for each man. The cavalry have ten rounds of ball and thirty of blank cartridges in the spring, and twenty rounds of blank in the winter.

The ball practice is conducted differently in different regiments; in some, the men fire under the superintendence of the captain of the company, one square at a time, and only five rounds each man. Every shot that is put into the target is carefully marked. In other regiments, the whole company goes out together; they fire from right to left, and get over it as soon as possible. The first method, if the practice was sufficient, and the best shots were rewarded, would surely teach the men in time to become good marksmen, provided the target is removed at times to a less or greater distance, so that they may ascertain the range of their pieces. The latter method is perfectly useless, and the firing might as well be with blank cartridges. The greatest number of rounds of ball cartridges for each man being only thirty for the year, except for light infantry, is totally inadequate to teach the men the real use of their weapon. From want of practice, and from having a musket so clumsy, and recoiling so much, the men are exceedingly nervous when they do practise ball firing in sections, subdivisions, or in companies two deep. There are not above two shots out of twenty that hit the mark; many of the muskets frequently go off before the word is given, and often before they have reached the men's shoulders. The recoil is so great, that the cheek is often bruised by it. The pouch is so inconvenient, that the men take several cartridges out at once, and tuck them in between the buttons of their coats in front, from which place they are easily knocked out, both unintentionally and intentionally; for from the dislike the men have to ball practice, they are glad to get rid of the ammunition in any way. The supernumeraries in the rear frequently pick up cartridges, when the men move off the ground, which have been lost or thrown away. When the ammunition in the pouch is nearly expended, and only a few cartridges remain, there is great difficulty in getting them out, as from the position of the pouch the men can hardly get their fingers into it, and are obliged to be helped by their neighbours. The barrel of the musket cannot be removed from the stock by the soldier to be cleaned, in the manner in which a fowling-piece is; consequently, the works of the lock are liable to injury from the water used in cleaning the barrel. The men frequently neglect to bite off the end of the cartridge, and sometimes when they have done so, they place the unbitten end downwards. After a regiment has been at practice, the serjeant-major always has a squad of men whose muskets will not go off from the above cause, and three and four cartridges are sometimes drawn from one musket, the first having been put in unbitten.

When the men move at double quick, the cross belts flap about a great deal; and the breast strap of the knapsack-belts confines the chest so much, and is so distressing to the men, that they invariably unbuckle it when marching. The bayonet is sheathed with difficulty, in consequence of the position of the scabbard; and when the knapsack is on, the soldier can scarcely return it without the assistance of another, probably a man of the rear rank.

This is a sad report of the method of teaching the soldier how to use the only weapons he has for defence and for offence. It appears that the musket is so heavy, so unwieldy, and recoils so much, that the men dread to use it. They seem to be always taught to fire on the same level as the target, never varying it down steeps, or up acclivities, nor across pieces of water; as if the enemy was always to be met on the same level ground as themselves, and never to be fired at when on higher or lower ground. Troops cannot be taught to use their muskets in this way. Our battalions are most of them exceedingly well drilled; they move with precision, and understand the various formations perfectly. These movements, however, are of little use, if the men are armed with muskets with which they cannot hit a mark. Indeed their movements may only place them in positions where they will become an easier sacrifice to the slaughtering fire of a well-armed enemy.

It is not right that a great nation like England should not arm her gallant troops with a musket that would put them on an equality with other European nations. The value of 100 balls does not much exceed one shilling; this is certainly the very smallest number that each soldier should fire in the year. But supposing that each man should cost 2s. in the year, and 30,000 men were to practise at this rate, it would cost 3000l. for teaching our soldiers the use of their arms. Can England afford this?

There is scarcely a part of our soldiers' dress, equipment, and arms that does not require alteration.

The present heavy cavalry helmet is made so top-heavy by a high plume, that it will with difficulty stay on the head when the troops move at a rapid pace; and they cannot well do the sword exercise when the plume is on it.

The lancer cap is nearly the worst that ever was invented, has the same objection on account of its height and plume, and does not in the least protect the back of the head from a blow of the sabre.

The hussar cap, though made of a good material, has all the prevailing objections that the others have.

The present infantry cap is kept on the head with great difficulty when the men move at double quick, by constantly putting one hand to it, in spite of which it frequently falls off.

The coatee is altogether a bad dress; it is made too tight, and is so cut away that it does not in the least cover the hips. The lace on it is very objectionable; it must be cleaned with pipeclay, which causes the cloth to wear out much sooner than it otherwise would, by the constant brushing necessary to keep it decent.

The trousers given to the men are made of very inferior cloth, and those which they provide themselves in summer are not what they ought to be. The white trousers formerly worn were very properly given up because the men cleaned them with wet pipeclay, and frequently put them on before they were dry, which produced sickness. The evil, unfortunately, is not yet remedied; for the men still clean their summer trousers with some wet process.

Hair-powder, pomatum, and great tails, tight white breeches and long black gaiters have vanished; but the tight stock remains. To encircle the soldier's neck with a band so stiff that he cannot turn his head without pain and difficulty, appears exceedingly absurd; for with his head so fettered it is impossible that he can carry his sight along the barrel of the musket so as to take correct aim.

Dr. William Fergusson writes, in his "Notes and Recollections of a Professional Life," "The circulation of the ascending arteries in the neck is by far the closest of any part of the human body, and to impede its relief by the returning veins, which a stiff ligature of any kind is sure to do, must have a stupifying effect on the brain. It cannot fail, besides, to deteriorate the sight, from the pressure of congested blood upon the optic nerve; and the stock would seem to be preserved only for the purpose of generating a tendency to all kinds of apoplectic and ophthalmic diseases. A tight ligature, not only on the neck, but any where else, should be rejected for ever from military dress and equipment of whatever description."

The feather and plume have been very properly discarded from the infantry soldiers' cap: they were neither useful nor ornamental, but exceedingly inconvenient.

Our cavalry continue, however, to wear very high plumes. Why is this? They are inconvenient to men on foot, how much more so must they be to mounted men. The footman cannot move very fast, and a feather interferes but little with his weapon; but the horseman, whose pace is frequently rapid, and in the charge excessively so, absolutely cannot keep a high helmet or cap, loaded with a ponderous plume, on his head. Neither a lancer or swordsman can execute all the movements of their weapons under such a head-dress. Moreover, the man's attention, required to keep different parts of his dress and equipment in their places, is withdrawn from its proper objects—the appliance of his weapon and the guidance of his horse. At the same time his seat in the saddle is shaken, and his power consequently diminished.

The following fact will show the effect of placing on the horseman's head a high helmet. Not long before the King's Dragoon Guards went to Canada, the regiment was inspected at Brighton by the late Lieutenant-General Sir Charles Dalbiac, who was then Inspector-General of Cavalry. It was to be reviewed on the Downes. Previous to turning out, the commanding officer, who was a very stout man, and resisted the air very much when mounted on a large horse, sent a message to the inspector-general to say, that the wind was high, and he thought the men would not be able to keep the helmets on their heads, and hoped they might be allowed to wear their forage caps! How could such a helmet as is shown in Plate XXXVII. possibly be kept on the head of any man in a high wind, mounted or dismounted? Next in absurdity to such a helmet as this, is the lancer cap.

We must not overlook the mustache as part of military costume; it is worn by our cavalry, but the infantry are shaved to a hair. What good reason is there for this? If it is considered warlike, are not our infantry warriors? If it is handsome, do not our infantry require it? If it is useful, to no troops can it be more so than to those who garrison our coldest and our hottest colonies, where the cutting cold of Canada cracks, and the vertical sun of India blisters the lips. Why the troops exposed to these severities should be deprived of what bountiful nature has provided for their protection, is difficult to understand. Shaving is always a disagreeable operation; in the field before the enemy it is frequently impracticable. If the articles which are carried expressly for this purpose could be got rid of, the soldier's load would be somewhat lightened. To propose that the soldier should wear his beard, would be called unenglish, outlandish, and various other hard names; it would, nevertheless, be a great comfort to the soldier, save him some trouble, protect his chin from the inclemency of the seasons, and render the stock round his neck quite unnecessary.

MARCHING.

It is needless to observe, that the most efficient armies are those which are armed and equipped the best, which can move the quickest, march the farthest, and fire the truest. The fate of nations has been decided by the rapid movements of armies, without fighting; and it may be so again. It is, then, of vast importance to us, that our gallant soldiers should be so armed, equipped, and clothed, that the utmost celerity of movement, and the greatest endurance in marching, may be acquired. These can only be attained by constant practice; and it is essential that the soldier should not be overloaded by the weight of his arms or the contents of his knapsack, and that his clothes should fit him easily and comfortably, without restraining his limbs in any way. If extra weight is carried, it is more desirable that it should be in his knapsack than elsewhere; for good clothes tend much towards good health, and in case of emergency, troops can be pushed on without their knapsacks, which can follow by other means.

A system much to be reprobated has of late years become usual with our infantry, that of moving from one quarter to another by railway instead of marching, the object of which is a saving of expense, a saving of the wear and tear of clothing, and an easier way for the men: but it is quite overlooked that this method prevents the men from acquiring one of the most essential duties of the infantry soldier—that of marching. It is true, that regiments have orders, when in quarters, to go out in heavy marching order two or three times a week, but there are many circumstances which may prevent the regularity of this practice, such as bad weather and dirty roads: but even when punctual on these little walking excursions, of perhaps five miles out and back again, they are very unlike real marching. On these occasions the soldiers seldom pack up the whole of their kitts, preferring to risk the chance of detection to being burthened with the weight of a full knapsack. War brings with it a succession of difficulties, hardships, and privations to the soldier; and though it would be unwise and cruel to visit him with evils as long as they can be avoided, yet, if he is to know how to conduct himself under them when they do exist, he should be practised in some of the inconveniences. Troops should not be sent by railway except in cases of emergency, but march by regular stages from one quarter to another. A march from Portsmouth to Edinburgh would teach a soldier more than he can ever learn by merely walking out from his barracks twice or three times a week. He would move day after day ten or fifteen miles, regardless of cold, wet, or heat, and whether the roads were clean or dirty: at the termination of each day's march he would have to seek his quarters, clean his arms and appointments, and get his food; besides which he would take his turn of mounting various guards. He would then discover all the errors of his dress and equipment, and the best method of carrying his knapsack; and speedily find out if that important part of a foot soldier's dress, the shoes, were calculated for long marches. The officers would become perfectly acquainted with all the imperfections that existed in the men's clothing, which, when properly reported to high authorities, would no doubt be rectified. Nobody but practical men can ascertain these points, nor should any persons attempt to invent any parts of equipment, and particularly the construction and method of carrying the knapsack, without consulting experienced and intelligent privates on the subject. The quotation already made from Marshal Saxe's "Memoirs," cannot be too often repeated, "that when a state so far degenerates as to suffer the discipline of its troops to be neglected, *or convenience to supply the place of use,* one may venture to foretell, without the gift of prophecy, that its ruin is approaching." It was so with Rome, it has been so with other nations. Let us take warning; for what has happened once may happen again!

Although the discipline of our army is not relaxed, and our men are no doubt as robust and brave as ever, yet there is an alarm at this moment about invasion, and a general feeling exists that our troops are not equipped and armed sufficiently well to meet any of the continental armies on fair terms. This feeling does not dwell only in the breasts of those who, from their professions or pursuits, may not be considered competent judges, but the press has of late been urgent on this subject; numerous letters have been inserted written by experienced and talented officers. Amongst others, Lieutenant-Colonel E. Napier's observations are worthy of notice, contained in an article of the "United Service Magazine" for the month of September, 1851, entitled "Proposed Alterations in our Military Dress, Arms, and Equipment." Not only are our soldiers unpractised in marching distances, but both officers and men have little or no opportunities of learning extended movements in the field beyond what can be taught in a barrack yard. It should be no matter of surprise, then, that our officers, never having manœuvred any force beyond the strength of a battalion, should feel embarrassed when in command of a large body of troops. There are very few garrisons in the United Kingdom where a brigade of infantry can be formed. And as to cavalry, there are but few quarters where a whole regiment is united. And yet we hear exclamations of surprise that in case of war we should have the greatest difficulty in finding an officer to command that arm. Of course we should, unless heaven-born generals can be found; for English cavalry generals receive no instruction on earth. Cavalry is by far the most difficult arm to handle: nothing but the constant practice of moving considerable bodies can teach an officer. Where, then, is our school for forming cavalry generals? With the finest men and the best horses in the world, our cavalry are always making mistakes.

In Germany and France a number of regiments of all arms are frequently assembled for the purpose of practising manœuvres on an extended scale, by which officers and men are taught the most important part of their profession. Why should England neglect her troops? There is an old saying, "that if any thing is worth having, it is worth having good." Surely it is false economy to have any machine that is not adapted to the purpose for which it has been framed.

England is now so intersected with railways, that almost any force of infantry can, in case of emergency, be rapidly assembled at any named point. The system of dispersing them throughout the kingdom is, therefore, no longer necessary. It is most desirable and fair that both officers and men should have an opportunity of learning their profession on a more extended scale; and for this purpose a considerable force should always be together in a central spot of England. Perhaps a better one cannot be named than Weedon, where considerable barracks are already built, and an enlargement only would be necessary. This place is not far distant from the populous towns of Birmingham and Manchester, and close to Northampton; to any one of which places troops could be sent from Weedon in a very short time: and if they should be required, they could reach the coast with little delay. Here, then, should be assembled, for the instruction and efficiency of the army, and more particularly for the formation of officers, a force consisting of not less than one troop of horse artillery, one brigade of foot artillery, two regiments, forming a brigade of cavalry; four battalions of infantry, forming two brigades; and one regiment of rifles. Then officers and men might form some idea of what an army is in the field, and learn what they never can in the barrack yard. This is but a small force, but it would be sufficient for the purpose. A hall of instruction, with a library, might be established, where officers would improve their minds and study the art of war. This proposition would probably be rejected on the score of expense, in spite of the advantages likely to accrue from it. The first expense, that of constructing barracks, would no doubt be considerable; but when completed other barracks would be abandoned, and might be sold. In many other respects it is likely that expenses would be saved. In the barrack establishments particularly. Government cannot be too strenuous in the encouragement of military men to become masters of their profession, and to divert both officers and privates, by every means in its power, from the idleness and ennui of a barrack life. This suggestion is made on the conviction that such an assemblage of troops is necessary, if our army is to be properly instructed and kept on an equality with the continental armies, where every improvement is speedily adopted.

FORMATION OF THE ARMY.

Now let us reflect on the present formation of the British army.

The governments on the Continent, whose armies are formed of troops of different nations, can scarcely avoid having them armed and dressed in various ways. It would be unwise to alter the arms and equipment of men accustomed to them from youth, being well skilled in the use of their weapons, and prejudiced in favour of their national dress. The armies of Austria and Russia are formed of different nations in various costumes. When Napoleon was Emperor of the French, his enormous army was composed of many nations, in a variety of dresses. England at an early period brought armies into the field clothed in many fantastic ways, and with a great variety of arms; this did not arise from their being formed of men of different nations, but from the manner in which the soldiers were recruited. The forces were raised principally by individuals of rank and wealth, who received a certain amount of money from the king, and paid their followers wages, some of whom were clothed in their chief's livery; others at their own expense: this produced a variety of dresses. Then the numerous descriptions of arms required different kinds of troops to use them. In the cavalry there were the men-at-arms, clad in armour, mounted on the best horses, and considered the élite of the army—they were men of high caste: the troops armed with cross-bows were dressed in a peculiar way; they were men of some wealth, for it was an expensive weapon. There were arquebusiers, pikemen, and hobilers, all varying in dress; and, from the nature of their arms, there was some reason for it. The hobiler was a very inferior description of cavalry mounted on a bad horse. Some of the infantry, as well as the cavalry, were armed with the cross-bow, the arquebus, and the pike; besides which, there were archers carrying bows and arrows. This will account for the motley troops of those days, when there was no standing army. The men were raised by their chiefs to serve for a fixed time, or for a particular service, and when that time had expired, or the service was performed, they returned to their homes and resumed their former occupations.

England is now in a very different state; and though we cannot say that we have a standing army, for without an annual vote of Parliament it would cease to be, yet we may consider it a permanent one. It is composed indifferently of English, Scotch, and Irish, all trained in the same manner, carrying the same arms, and using them equally well. The horses of our cavalry differ a little in strength, but are all equally good, and of one description. The men are recruited from the same class of people, and though varying in weight, are all sufficiently strong, and equally brave and active; both heavy and light are instructed in outpost duties and in skirmishing, and are expected in the charge to overthrow any cavalry that can be brought against them. Their arms are lances, swords, carbines, and pistols. Our infantry are all armed with the musket and bayonet; the rifles with a rifle-piece. We have battalions of grenadiers, and battalions of light infantry, who carry the same arms as the other regiments of infantry, and are all taught the same manœuvres, and instructed in outpost and light infantry movements. They are all, without distinction, expected to bear the brunt of battle, and the one regiment ever has been, and ever will be, as forward in the fray as the other.

Now, as there is no difference in the duties of our cavalry, and those of our infantry are all the same (the rifles always excepted), taking in turn our Colonial service, why should there continue a distinction in dress? In the cavalry we have dragoon guards and dragoons, carbineers and hussars, differently dressed, and, in some points, differently equipped, but armed with the same weapons, and performing the same duties. In the infantry we have grenadiers, who no longer carry grenades; and we have fusileers, who are no longer armed with the fusil. We have no inferior troops. Will the hussars allow themselves to be compared with hobilers, and say they are unfit to charge an enemy? Will the light infantry allow that they are not equal to the stand-up fight in line? Certainly not; there cannot be better troops than our hussars, there cannot be finer than our light infantry. We all know how distinguished they both were during the Peninsular war, at the commencement of which, heavy and light dragoons were brigaded together; they did outpost duty together, they skirmished together, and they charged and overthrew Napoleon's best troops together. They endured all the hardships of that war with the same unflinching resolution, and they emulated each other by the same determined bravery; there was no difference except in dress. Of the infantry exactly the same may be said.

As there no longer exists, then, any good reason why troops using the same arms, and performing the same duties, should not wear the same dress, it is surely time to get rid of every thing that in any way interferes with the use of the soldier's weapon, or shakes the firmness of the horseman's seat. We should remove from the infantry grenadiers wings and grenades on their equipment, from light infantry the wings, and from these and all other regiments the white cotton tape, which is put on in almost as many varied ways as there are regiments in the service, to the great annoyance of the soldier, who must clean it with pipeclay and brush, to the injury of the cloth, and to the disgust of almost all military men.

It is clear, then, that there is no plea for a variety of dress; that garb which is well adapted to the duties of one mounted man, is so for another. The best dress for one footman is the best dress for the other, where their duties and arms are precisely the same. All our cavalry, except the Household Brigade, should be light cavalry; all our infantry, light infantry and riflemen. Distinctions in the dress of different regiments are very objectionable; they create jealousy without answering any good purpose; they are not the proper distinctions for conspicuous valour or good conduct.

The British soldier values highly the decoration of a medal; but to distribute them to every officer and private of a regiment, or to every man engaged in any general battle, defeats the object by destroying the distinction. At the battle of Waterloo, in spite of the general gallant bearing of our victorious army, there were amongst the troops, and indeed, sad to say, amongst the officers, several cowards! but they received medals as well as the bravest. No doubt, in the late bloody battles on the Sutledge, many instances could be recorded where medals were not deserved. If whole regiments are to be marked with favour, there should be a *corps élite* formed of distinguished officers and men who have been decorated with medals, and who might enjoy a small increase of pay, and certain privileges; but if there are objections to the formation of such a corps, still the decoration for bravery should only hang on the breasts of those who have earned it. It has been said that the French soldier is quicker than the British soldier; this probably only originates in the difference of training. The latter is far more enduring, patient, and obedient; his glory and position is that of a fair stand-up fight, without passion or loss of temper. If worsted, he can retire from the contest without the feeling of utter defeat; but he will sustain it as long or longer than any other warrior of ancient or modern times. When in actual presence of the enemy, his bearing is majestic, courageous, magnanimous—silent withal, except when he utters the battle-shout in closing with the bayonet. His sense of honour is as high, and will not brook inferiority to any adversary that can be placed before him. Of vain-glory he has none; and he is often a hero without knowing it, for he will perform the most daring actions as if they were in the ordinary routine of his duty, without uttering a boast or preferring a claim. Such is the general character of the British soldier. Of course it is not always sustained. Gallant deeds in the field of battle, whether performed with a victorious or defeated army, are still gallant deeds, and sometimes of more value in a retreat than on the advance: they should be rewarded by a decoration.

The term military, with regard to dress, is frequently very erroneously applied; the impression on most minds of what is so, is made by the dress they have been accustomed to see on soldiers, without considering if such dress is adapted to the purposes of war. A cap, for instance, such as our lancers wear, though rich and brilliant in appearance, and decorated with a waving plume, does not protect the head from the blow of a sabre when on, and certainly will not do so when off, where it is almost sure to be in a rapid charge. Such a cap is not adapted to war, and therefore should not be considered military. Let us refer to the soldiers of Elizabeth's time, in Plate XIX.: are those big breeches military? Are those still larger, in Plate XX., military? Is that tall grenadier's cap, in Plate XXIX., military? Was the ponderous wig full of curls, falling over the shoulders, with a three-cornered cocked-hat on the top of it, military? All these in their time have been considered military; and they were quite as much so as many parts of the soldier's equipment of the present day. No part of dress, however, can be deemed military, nor should be put on a soldier, which in any way impedes his action, is inconvenient, uncomfortable, and not adapted to the purposes of war.

It has been suggested by a cavalry officer in command of a regiment, that the heavy cavalry should be dressed in a short surtout coat, and the light dragoon in a round jacket. Why this distinction? How erroneous the proposition! If we are to have heavy and light dragoons, the outpost duties of course fall to the lot of the latter, and then they require the skirted coat. Surely it must be most wanted by those most exposed to the inclemencies of the weather, which the light dragoons would be; while the heavier, reserved for the brunt of battle, would be kept in quarters. But if these troops are armed in the same way, that which is an appropriate dress for one horseman is so for another. Of all the annoying devices that have been invented for a cavalry officer, aiguillettes and epaulettes are the most so; they perfectly cripple him when mounted; and the scales on the privates' shoulders are found to be exceedingly inconvenient, cramping the action of the arms, and of course diminishing the power of effectually using their weapons.

No remark has hitherto been made on the dress of the rifle corps; and it may be expected that it will escape censure. Not so, however, for the colour of their dress is not calculated for the purpose intended. While the line soldier should be bright and brilliant, the rifleman should be obscure: but our riflemen are too dark; they are almost black. Black, perhaps, may be considered an obscure colour, but it is much more conspicuous than many brighter colours. Browns of various shades, and not very dark, and greys, are much more invisible than the rifle-green.

It cannot escape the observation of any one, how wonderfully Providence has provided for the security of many animals, by the similarity of their colour to that of the ground. The hare, when perfectly still in her form, cannot be seen by the unpractised eye. The rabbit is also difficult to see; and so is the tiger in the jungle. There are birds also most difficult to discern when perfectly still on the ground; the partridge, the lark, and many others. None of these are black, nor are they very dark in colour; if they were, they would instantly be discovered; but their colours blend so with those of the ground, tufts of dry grass, and shrubs, that it requires great practice to detect them. So it should be with the rifleman, who takes up an eligible position to use his rifle with advantage behind a shrub, a mound, or hillock, or amongst underwood, and sometimes behind the stems of trees. Except when the smoke from the discharge of his rifle makes it evident where he is, he should be as secure from discovery as a hare or a partridge. He cannot be so in his present dress; the darkest foliage, even that of the yew-tree, is not so dark as his dress; scarcely so are the deepest shadows in a wood: the stems of trees are brown, and some, when the sun shines on them, are bright. The rifleman's dress, therefore, should be either brown or grey, and not dark. There were some of the Portuguese Caçadores dressed in brown during the Peninsular war, with black equipment. It was a handsome dress, but too dark, though better adapted to the purpose than the colour of our riflemen.

The cap of our lancer regiments has already been mentioned as very objectionable. There is no good reason why a horseman carrying a lance should be in a different dress from a horseman armed with the sword and carbine. The square pouch of the light dragoon was found to be in the way of the lance; therefore a flatter one was given to them;

and they required buckets to the stirrup-irons for the end of the lance to rest in. In other respects, any convenient dress for a mounted man is equally so for a lancer. It was absurd to put them into a foreign dress because foreigners carried the lance. The fact is, the lance is a heavy dragoon weapon, and not calculated for outpost duty.

Little has been written about the household troops, because they must be considered as separate from the rest of the army, having no Colonial duties to perform, and being always about the court. The cavalry brigade is magnificently appointed; and if their helmets were deprived of the plume, and the officers' coats of the epaulettes and aiguillettes, and the men's shoulders of the scales, when they wear the cuirass, they would be greatly improved. If brought fresh into the field, there are no troops in the world would stand before them.

The cap of the foot guards has been criticised. It is possible that they may admire and like it themselves; but if an enemy should land on our coasts, there would be much more required of these brave soldiers than mounting guard; and then, when too late, they would deplore being hampered with such a head-dress. They could not embark on active service in so unwarlike a cap.

If soldiers are wanted merely to enrich the pageant of state ceremonies, it is of little importance how they may be encumbered with rich, brilliant, and useless trappings. But if the British army is to be composed of warriors, the dress, arms, and equipment should be adapted to the purposes of war. The review dress should be the war dress; our troops should march from the review-ground to embark for active service, perfectly equipped at all points for that service, without the slightest alteration, always ready and efficient, without any decoration expressly for reviews.

Scarlet has been objected to as a bad colour for soldiers. No doubt it does not wear so well as many other coloured cloths; but it has been the national colour for a vast number of years; it has been worn in all our victories; it is known as the British colour all over the world; and there is no serious inconvenience in it. For troops of the line it is brilliant and imposing. It would be unwise to change it. But it is of vital importance to our army that the arms should be of the best description, and the dress and equipments perfectly adapted to the use of them.

The strength of the horseman consists in the united powers of two animals, directed by the skill of one of them, the rider. The nearer they can be brought to be like a centaur, the more formidable must they be. If the horse is overweighted, power is diminished; if the rider is armed with a bad weapon, he is not much to be feared. If he is clogged with tassels, strings, buckles, and straps, or any part of his equipment calls for his attention, and shakes him in his saddle, he is rendered of little value. The footman's power rests in the rapid and accurate fire of his musket; restrain the freedom of his limbs by unsuitable dress, or ill-adapted equipment, arm him with a weapon without teaching him how to use it, and he becomes himself useless. With regard to the dress of troops serving in our Colonies, there ought to be no difficulty. The climate of Canada as the coldest, and that of India as the hottest, are very well known; and we have plenty of experienced officers and men who know what dresses are best suited to them. Surely it would be better to have a fixed costume for different climates, than to leave the dress of regiments to the fancy of each commanding officer. In India, the white linen jacket and trowsers are perfectly suited to the climate; nothing can be cooler or more agreeable to wear in excessive heat; but many commanding officers set their faces against this dress, and distress the men by compelling them to wear cloth when the heat is almost insupportable. In the winter season of India cloth is necessary, the cold sometimes being severe.

One of the important parts of a foot soldier's equipment is his knapsack; various changes have been made in it from time to time, but none seem to have been quite successful. Practical men alone can decide on the most useful kind, or the best method of carrying it. At present, a strap across the chest, for the purpose of keeping the shoulder-straps in their places, is found to be so oppressive to the soldier, that he cannot march far without loosening it. The present knapsack, painted black, seems to be, in the opinion of most military men, very inferior to a knapsack made of an animal's skin, with the hair outwards.

If the costume of the Highland regiments is really a national costume, and it induces the Scotch to enlist in those regiments when they would not enlist in others, it may be a reason for continuing it; otherwise, there can scarcely be a more unserviceable dress.

Having criticised generally, and rather severely, the present dress of our army, their arms and equipments, and pointed out those parts which are most objectionable, and require change; having also deprecated the practice of sending our infantry by railways, instead of marching them from one quarter to another; and, moreover, disapproved of the formation of our army; the Author is anxious to impress on the mind of his readers, that his motives are the kindest feelings towards the army, and the most anxious wish to benefit both officers and privates, by inducing the authorities to arm, clothe, and equip them more efficiently, more for their general comfort, and at less expense to the officers.

To find fault is easy, but to correct errors is difficult; and to devise any thing perfectly suited to the purpose intended, is more so. Nevertheless, no improvement can take place until defects are detected. By the experience of the past we ought to benefit.

On reference to the drawings and descriptions of dresses in this volume, we may trace the various changes which have taken place while armour was worn, and the gradual disuse of it. Fire-arms, which were at first unwieldy, uncertain weapons, heavy to carry and slow to fire, superseded but gradually bows and arrows. This is not surprising, for our bowmen were very expert, and renowned throughout Europe; and it is hardly possible to conceive any thing more formidable than flights of thousands of well-directed arrows, carrying death into the ranks of the foe. The ease of holding a bow, and the rapidity with which arrows could be discharged, greatly retarded the general use of a lumbering matchlock; however, as they improved in make, the firelock was more esteemed, and at last the musketeer superseded the archer. It will be observed, that it was only on certain occasions of military pomp, that high crests and plumes, and inconvenient trappings, were introduced; but when the soldier took the field, he was defensively armed with close-fitting armour made as flexible as possible, and a helmet fitting firmly on his head. Cumbrous dress succeeded armour; heavy buff coats, enormous boots, and all the equipments, were unnecessarily weighty. Gradually they became lighter; and slowly some of the absurdities, such as enormous wigs, powder, pomatum, and tails, frills and ruffles, were left off, and the army became habited in a more tolerable costume.

For thirty-six years we have been reposing on the laurels gained at Waterloo, and have since then rather blinked military improvements; while on the Continent they have been alive to every new invention.

Although it is most desirable that the dress of the British army should be very different from that of all foreign armies (for this reason we should continue the scarlet), yet to borrow from them whatever may be truly valuable in arms, dress, or equipment, is quite right. Unfortunately, we are too apt to adopt every novelty we see, regardless of utility. We have introduced the large-topped, overweighted shako from the French; we have had the large trowser from the Cossack; the front of the coat padded and stuffed like the Russian. We have changed from one extreme to another, without good reason; and we have still tight coats, stiff stocks, high caps and tall plumes, all of which, it is to be hoped, for the comfort of our soldiers and the efficiency of our army, will shortly be got rid of.

Having endeavoured to show that there no longer exists any good reason for the great variety of dress which exists in our army, and with the feeling that its formation requires reorganization, it is proposed to reform both cavalry and infantry in the following manner:—to divide the cavalry into heavy and light dragoons, and the infantry into light infantry and rifles.

Our cavalry force at present consists of 26 regiments, thus divided:— 3 regiments of cuirassiers, 7 of dragoon guards, 3 of heavy dragoons, 4 of light dragoons, 4 of lancers, and 5 of hussars.

Our infantry force consists of 103 regiments, exclusive of Colonial regiments; but some of them have more than one battalion, amounting in all to 114 battalions; composed of 7 battalions of foot guards, 6 of fusileers, 9 of Highlanders, 7 of light infantry, 4 of riflemen, and 81 other battalions of the line.

It is proposed to reform the army as follows:—

The household brigade, consisting of 3 regiments of cuirassiers, to remain as at present.

3 regiments of cuirassiers, to be formed from the dragoon guards, and to be armed with lances, swords, and pistols.

20 regiments of light dragoons, to be formed of the remaining regiments of cavalry, all to be equipped and dressed in the same way, and to be armed with swords, carbines, and pistols. These regiments to take their turn of duty in India, as well as in all other parts of the world.

The infantry to be reformed thus:—

7 battalions of guards as at present.

20 battalions of rifles, to be formed by 9 battalions of Highlanders, 7 of light infantry, and 4 of the present rifles. The remaining 87 battalions to be all made light infantry; making the whole force to consist, as at present, of 114 battalions.

Three regiments of cuirassiers, armed with lances, would be irresistible. The lance is a heavy dragoon weapon, and not fit for outpost duty. Six regiments of cuirassiers are probably enough for our small army. The heaviest horses would, of course, be selected for these troops; but the light dragoons would, nevertheless, be sufficiently well mounted to oppose any cavalry in the world.

To designate 87 battalions "light infantry," cannot affect the strength or bravery of the individual soldier; and these battalions would be quite as formidable in line as grenadiers, and more serviceable for all other purposes. The term "grenadier" has no longer any meaning, but that of a tall man with a very high cap; it need, therefore, cause no regret if we lose it for ever.

We have lately discovered how very wanting our army is in riflemen; it is therefore proposed to increase them to 20 battalions. This number is not too many. No force should ever leave our shores without a proportion of riflemen with it. We have generally 20 or 21, sometimes more, battalions of infantry in India; 5 regiments of rifles would be but a fair proportion of that force; 3 battalions in Bengal, and one at each of the other presidencies. If we had had a rifle force with the army under Sir George Pollock when he forced the Khyber Pass on his advance to Cabul, we should have heard but little of the formidable jezail. Having thus reformed the army, the costume would be simplified, and that amazing variety, which is so useless, would be much diminished.

It is suggested that the life guards and blues should not be altered, excepting to remove the plume from the helmets, and the epaulettes and aiguillettes from the officers' shoulders when wearing the cuirass; and the scale from the privates' shoulders, giving them a simple strap.

The three regiments proposed to be made cuirassiers, to wear scarlet frock coats, single-breasted, straps on the shoulders, cuffs and collars the colour of the facing of the regiment; grey trowsers, with stripes on the outside seams of yellow lace; Wellington boots, with spurs to the heels; steel helmets, with brass ornaments, without plumes or feathers. Arms—lances, straight three-edged swords, and pistols.

The officers.—Scarlet frock coats the same cut as the privates', gold straps on the shoulders. The rank of the officers to be distinguished by bands of lace round the cuffs: a field-officer to have three, a captain two, a subaltern one. Epaulettes to be worn only in full dress on foot, without the cuirass; never to be worn mounted; steel helmets, with brass ornaments; grey trowsers with stripes down the outside seams of gold lace: the same for dress. The coat without epaulettes to be the undress. Arms—long straight three-edged sharp-pointed swords, and pistols.

Twenty regiments of light dragoons.—Blue frock coats, double-breasted, straps on the shoulders, cuffs and collars the colour of the facings of the regiments; grey trowsers, stripes down the outside seams of yellow lace; Wellington boots, spurs fixed to the heels; helmets, black with brass ornaments, to be made of a material which will not be too heavy, at the same time strong, and will not be affected by the sun or wet. No plumes or feathers. Arms—carbines, sabres, and pistols.

Officers' dress.—Coats of the same cut as the men's, gold straps on the shoulders. The rank to be distinguished by bands of lace round the cuffs, as described for the cuirassier. Epaulettes to be worn in full dress when dismounted, but never when mounted. Trowsers for dress and undress the same, grey, with stripes down the outside seams of gold lace. Arms—sabres and pistols.

The horse artillery might be the same as the light dragoons.

Eighty-seven battalions of light infantry.—Surtout coats, scarlet, double-breasted, straps on the shoulders, cuffs and collars the colour of the facing of the regiment; grey trowsers, with stripes down the outside seams of yellow lace; helmets black, with bronze ornaments, without plumes or feathers; short gaiters and shoes. The pouches to run on straps round the waist, so that they can be carried behind or before at pleasure. The bayonets to hang from the waist belts, either on the right or left side, as may be most convenient for drawing and returning them. The pouches will, of course, traverse on the opposite side: this will relieve the shoulders from all weight, except that of the knapsacks, and provisions when carried, which is enough for that part of the body. The coats to be made sufficiently roomy to admit of a warm waistcoat with sleeves in cold weather. Arms—good detonating muskets and bayonets.

The officers.—Scarlet surtout coats of the same cut as the privates', gold straps on the shoulders, cuffs and collars the colour of the facings of the regiment. The rank to be distinguished by bands of lace round the cuffs. Epaulettes to be worn when in full dress, but never in the field when with the troops. Trowsers grey, with gold lace down the outside seams. Helmets black, with bronze ornaments. Straight swords with sharp points.

Riflemen.—Grey surtout coats, double-breasted, of a light shade; trowsers a light brown or dark drab colour, with black stripes down the outside seams; short gaiters and shoes; helmets in shape like the light infantry, but in colour the same as the trowsers, a light brown or dark drab, with bronze ornaments, without plumes or feathers.

Lieutenant-Colonel E. Napier, in his proposed alterations in our military dress, &c., recommends a horse-hair plume on a movable pivot coming out of the top of the helmet, as a shelter against the rays of the sun. Surely this would greatly increase the top weight of the helmet; and the slightest breeze would blow it on one side, so as to expose the helmet to the sun. A plume is, moreover, in every respect an inconvenient and bad ornament for a soldier's head-dress. The best protection from the rays of the sun is a highly-glazed linen case for the helmet: if it is wadded with cotton, it will be more perfect: white is probably the best, but if it is highly glazed the colour is not of so much importance.

It is most desirable to get rid of the stiff leather stock worn by the privates. A smooth piece of brown leather, sewn inside of the collar of the coat, sufficiently stiff to prevent the collar from sinking down, would render any stock or neckcloth unnecessary. The throat is much less liable to disease by being kept cool, than when encircled by a warm neckcloth, which first creates perspiration and afterwards causes cold.

With regard to the construction of military caps, there are two excellent materials which seldom seem to be used for that purpose; one is light wicker-work, the other is cork. The latter is very light, is a non-conductor of solar heat, impervious to water, and hardly possible to be cut through with a sabre.

It is proposed that the officers should have but one description of coat, which is made full dress by adding epaulettes, and undress by merely wearing gold straps on the shoulders. This will be a great saving of expense; and when officers change their regiments, the facings and buttons will only have to be altered. Nothing can be more agreeable to wear than the frock coat, and with epaulettes on the shoulders it will be rich and handsome.

XLVII.

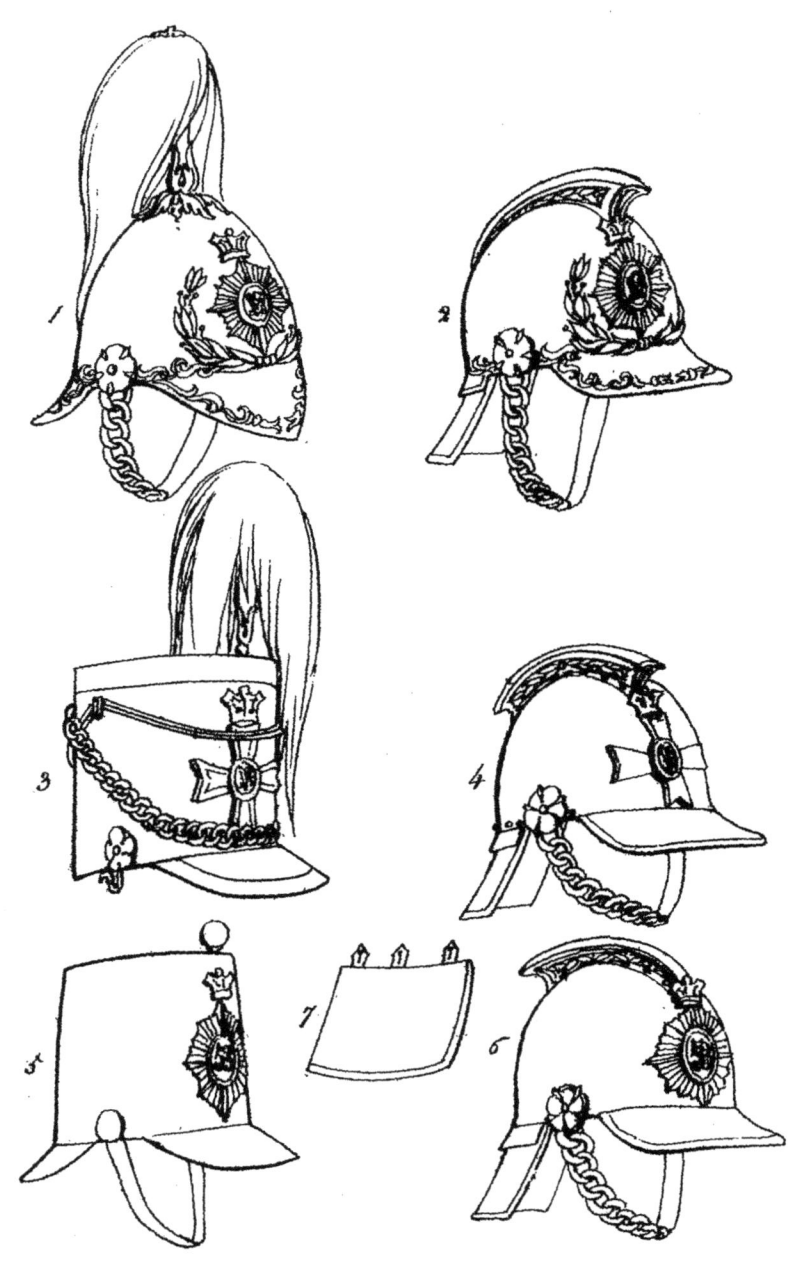

A D 1852.

PLATE XLVII.

IN this Plate there are pourtrayed, the present head-dresses of our army, and those proposed.

No. 1, is the helmet lately decided on for the heavy cavalry. It has two great defects: the first is the plume, which is in every sense of the word, as already explained, most objectionable for a horseman; the second is the peak, which, coming to a point almost like the head of a salmon, is not well calculated to protect both eyes from the glare of the sun; and it is brought down in continuation of the curve of the head-piece, which brings it so near the nose, that the wearer cannot see straight before him without throwing back his head or his helmet.

No. 2, is a helmet proposed for the cuirassiers.

No. 3, is the present cap of the light dragoons, of which there are only four regiments in the army; the others, though called light dragoons, are lancers and hussars. The objections to this cap are, its height and the plume; and there is no protection to the back of the head. It is, nevertheless, a better head-dress than the lancer or hussar cap, both of which are equally without the slightest protection to the back of the head: the lancer cap is shown in Plate XXXVI., also in Plate XXXVII., and again in Plate XXXIX.; and in the latter Plate the hussar cap is also drawn.

No. 4, is a helmet proposed for all our light dragoons.

No. 5, is one of our present infantry caps: they are exceedingly objectionable, because the men cannot keep them on their heads, and they are also devoid of protection behind.

No. 6, is proposed for our infantry.

The present heavy dragoon helmet, and the infantry cap, have a small peak behind, which is for the purpose of keeping the rain out of the neck; and it may also be intended for the protection of the back of the head from the cut of a sabre; but it will not answer either for the one or for the other purpose. Moreover, it can be but of little avail as to protection in the infantry cap, as the material of the cap itself can be cut through with the greatest facility any where, except straight down from the top. It is therefore proposed to have a shifting-guard for the back of the head and neck, which would hang on to three buttons under the small projection behind, shown in the helmets, figs. 2, 4, and 6. This guard is represented by fig. 7: it should be made of the same material as the helmet, and lined with soft leather, hanging by three small leather straps. It would always be on the helmet during a march and when in the field, but need not be used in fine weather, when in quarters. It will perfectly protect the back of the head and neck from a sabre cut, and as perfectly keep the rain out of the neck.

With regard to the shape of these proposed helmets, they vary but little. They are ornamented on the front with the same devices as the present helmets and caps. They can be made either of metal or any other material calculated for the purpose, and of any colour, if not made of polished steel. Polished steel is very brilliant in appearance, but it is troublesome to keep bright, and if made sufficiently thick to protect the head from a sabre cut, becomes too heavy; it is therefore necessary to make it of thin plates of steel, and have transverse bars, either inside or outside, to strengthen it.

There seems to be no good reason why a helmet adapted to cavalry should not be equally so to infantry, provided it is not too heavy. There is no difference in the shape of that proposed for infantry and those for cavalry, except in the bar which passes over the crest. Fig. 6, is perhaps the handsomest of the three. The shape of these helmets surely is handsomer than the helmets and caps drawn opposite to them, and if properly made, would be most comfortable to wear, and adapted to the purpose intended. We have now become reconciled to

XLVIII.

the infantry cap without feather or plume, and should think them unmilitary if again worn: very soon should we feel exactly the same regarding the plumes of the cavalry; and if, fortunately, they should be discarded, it is not likely that they will ever be resumed.

Plate XLVIII.

In the foreground of this Plate is a private of infantry in the proposed dress. In the background are an officer and a private; the former in the dress in which officers should always appear on parade, without epaulettes; the latter is in marching order, with his pouch brought to the front, which would be its position in battle. A broad leather belt should be worn round the waist, to which the pouch could be attached by a runner, so that it can at pleasure be brought to the front or rear. Both the belt and pouch must be constructed for the purpose. The bayonet at present is hung on the left side; but it admits of a doubt if the method now practised of fixing it is the best; it is possible that it would be more readily fixed and unfixed, and returned to its scabbard, if suspended on the right side; if so, the pouch could pass from the rear to the front, and back again, as easily on the other side. The man in marching order is represented with the strap across the chest, as at present worn; but it is very desirable that some better method of carrying the knapsack should be invented, as the strap above-mentioned is found to be very painful to the chest.

This dress has nothing about it that can in any way incommode the wearer. The helmet would sit firmly on the head, without top weight; it is high enough to prevent concussion from a blow, and to admit sufficient air within; it may be black, with brass ornaments, or with bronze ornaments, or made of any colour. Steel is too troublesome to keep clean, and too hot for tropical climates.

Plate XLIX.

In this Plate three officers in full dress are represented; one of cuirassiers, without the cuirass, another of light dragoons, and the third of infantry.

Plate L.

In this last drawing are represented a cuirassier dismounted, armed with lance and long straight sword; in the distance is a light dragoon.

It may, perhaps, be more desirable to have six regiments of heavy dragoons armed with lances, than three regiments of cuirassiers, by which the expense of cuirasses would be saved, and the regiments be more generally useful. Under these circumstances, there would be a saving of expense in the proposed dresses; for the only increase would be in additional cloth for the skirts of the soldiers' coats, while a considerable diminution in expense would take place by getting rid of plumes, cap-lines, shoulder-scales, and the hussar dress in the cavalry; and shoulder-wings, white tape, and the heavy cross belts, with brass plates on them, in the infantry. Both cavalry and infantry would then be more comfortably and more efficiently clad. The difference of expense, however, in the one dress or the other, is not worth a consideration. England can surely afford to dress her troops in the best manner; and the most appropriate is the most economical method.

XLIX.

L.

EXPLANATION OF VARIOUS PARTS OF ARMOUR.

IT is not improbable that there are terms used in the preceding pages, relative to armour, with which many persons are not familiar; an explanation, therefore, may be desirable.

OF HELMETS.

A close helmet entirely covers the head, face, and neck, having in front perforations to admit air, and slits through which to see. This part is called the visor, and lifts up by means of pivots over each ear. Some close helmets have what is called a bever, which, when closed, covers the mouth and chin, and either lifts up with the visor, or lets down by means of two pivots over the chin; it consists of two laminæ or plates shutting one over the other. Helmets with bevers are rare; the use of them was to enable the wearer to eat and drink with greater ease than could be done with a visor only. The helmets of the Greeks and Romans were mostly, if not always, open. The Grecian helmets in the British Museum have a guard for the nose, called a nasal. Helmets were divided into different kinds, called chapelle de fer, burgonet, bascinet, skull or hufden, castle, pot, and morion.

Chapelle de Fer—means iron hat. Chapelle formerly meant every kind of covering for the head. Chapelles de fer are on the heads of some of our kings in their seals. The chapelle de fer mentioned by Froissart as the head-piece of the light horse and foot soldiers, was a light head-dress, different from the first mentioned.

The Bourgenot or Burgonet.—Monsieur Fauchet says, when helmets better represented the human head, they were called bourguinotes, probably from being invented by the Burgundians. Figs. 10 and 14, in Plate XV., are burgonets. No. 4, in Plate XXV., is also a burgonet.

EXPLANATION OF VARIOUS PARTS OF ARMOUR.

The Bascinet—was a light helmet, so called from its likeness to a basin, generally without a visor; but the visor was sometimes added. It was worn in the reigns of Edward II. and III., and Richard II., by most of the English infantry.

The Salade—was a sort of light casque, without a crest; they were of different forms; sometimes they had visors. Nos. 7 and 8, in Plate XV., are salades.

The Skull—was a head-piece, without a visor or bever, like a bowl or basin.

The Hufden—was a head-piece something like the skull; it was worn by archers; it is mentioned in Queen Elizabeth's time.

The Castle—was a close head-piece; a corruption, probably, from the French word casquetel, a small light helmet.

The Morion—a kind of open helmet, without visor or bever, somewhat resembling a hat. It was commonly worn by arquebusiers and musquetiers. Nos. 1 and 2, in Plate XXV., are morions.

The Pot—was an iron hat with a broad rim. Figs. 3 and 6 are pots, in Plate XXV., though they do not differ much from morions.

Pileus.—A cap worn by the Romans, something like our night-cap. It is often seen on medals; it was given to the slaves on their gaining freedom, who were then called liberti, and thence became the symbol of freedom. Suetonius, speaking of the great joy the people of Rome had at the death of Nero, says, they ran about the city with the pileus on their heads.

Apex.—A light Roman cap, with a rod in the middle of it.

Tutulus.—A Roman cap, lined with woollen, and in the form of a cone.

Galerus.—A Roman cap made of the skins of victims.

Petasus.—A cap used by travellers, worn in Greece and Rome. Alexander the Great at feasts wore the petasus; it had a rim or margin narrower than modern hats. The figure of Mercury is frequently represented with it, ornamented with wings.

DESCRIPTION OF DEFENSIVE ARMOUR FOR THE BODY.

PLATE MAIL—consisted of a number of small laminæ of metal, commonly iron, laid one over the other like scales of fish, and sewed on to a strong leathern jacket.

The Hauberk—was a complete covering of mail from head to foot, consisting of a hood joined to a jacket, with sleeves, breeches, stockings, and shoes of double chain mail, to which were added gauntlets. Some hauberks opened before, some behind.

The Haubergeon—was a coat composed either of plate or chain mail, without sleeves.

The Jazeraunt or Jazerine—was a jacket strengthened with plate. It is mentioned in ancient romances, but there is no specific description of it.

The Aketon—was a quilted leathern jacket worn under the armour. In the romance of Alexander (fourteenth century) a knight is pierced "through brunny and shield to the *akedoun*."

In a wardrobe account of the time of John, in the Harleian Library, No. 4573, is an entry " for a pound of cotton to stuff an aketon for the king," which cost twelve pence ; and the same amount was expended in quilting it. The aketon was worn by the English infantry. The gambeson, or wambasium, seems to have been something of the same kind ; it was a quilted tunic, stuffed with wool, fitting the body, and worn under the haubergeon.

The Cuirass.—Armour for the breast and back, consisting of two parts, united at the sides of the body. They were originally made of leather, whence cuirace, or cuir, *i.e.* leather. Some may have been made of cuir-bouilly, a manufacture of boiled leather, which was very hard and durable, and was used in the middle ages for various parts of armour.

The Halecret—was a kind of corselet of two pieces, lighter, but something like the cuirass.

The Brigandine—takes its name from troops on the Continent by which it was first worn, who were called brigands; they were a light-armed, irregular force, much addicted to plunder. The brigandine consisted of a number of small plates of iron sewed upon quilted leather, a good defence to the body against the sword and pike. There are several in the Tower. The archers in Plate XIX. wear them.

Almaine-Rivets.—It is difficult to discover the exact form of them. They were overlapping plates held together by rivets, for the lower part of the body, and were of foreign make. In the reign of Henry VIII., a person, by name Guido Portavarii, merchant of Florence, agreed to furnish 2000 complete harness, called almaine-rivets, consisting of a salet, a gorget, a breastplate, a backplate, and a pair of splyntes, for the price of 16s. sterling.

Corslet.—A suit of armour, chiefly worn by pikemen. The word, strictly speaking, meant only that part covering the body, but was generally used to express the whole suit, including head-piece and gorget; the back and breast, with skirts of iron called tasses, or tassets, covering the thighs.

Pauldroons.—Pieces of armour for the shoulders.

Brassarts.—Plate armour for the upper part of the arm, reaching from the shoulder to the elbow, sometimes in a single piece, sometimes in a series of overlapping plates.

Splints.—Small overlapping plates for the defence of the bend of the arm; they constituted part of the suit called almaine-rivets.

Cuisses, or Cuissarts.—Strips of iron rivetted together for the protection of the thighs.

Genouillières—were flexible knee-pieces, with joints like those of a lobster.

Tapul.—The perpendicular ridge down the centre of a breastplate.

Tassets, or Taces.—Flexible plates, which were hooked on to the skirts of the cuirass.

Greeves.—Plate armour for the legs.

Sollerets.—The overlapping plates which formed the shoe of an armed knight.

ARMOUR FOR HORSES.

THE Chamfrien, or Chamfron.—Formed of copper, brass, or iron. It covered the front of the head, and had sometimes a spike projecting from the centre of the forehead. There were also demy-chamfrons, reaching only half way down the horse's head.

Crinère, or Manifère—consisted of a number of plates hooked together, placed down the mane, to guard the neck of the horse.

Poitrinal—was the buttock-piece; it descended nearly to the hocks.

A horse fully armed was said to be barded, frequently erroneously written barbed.

THE END.

www.ingramcontent.com/pod-product-compliance
Lightning Source LLC
Chambersburg PA
CBHW051040160426
43193CB00010B/1014